UNSPOKEN BEQUEST

*The Contribution
of German Jews
to German Culture*

Hugo Munsterberg

Raymond Saroff
PUBLISHER

UNSPOKEN BEQUEST

Published by Raymond Saroff, Publisher, Acorn Hill Road, Box 269, Olive Bridge, New York 12461. Designed by Bruce McPherson. Edited by Kathleen Hamel Peifer; copy edited by Robyn Pickering; picture research by Erica Blumenfeld. Typeset in Bembo by Studio Graphics, Kingston. Printed by Braun-Brumfield, Ann Arbor, on pH neutral paper. First edition.
1 3 5 7 9 10 8 6 4 2   1995 1996 1997 1998 1999 2000

Photography and illustration credits appear on page 264, and constitute a continuation of this copyright page.

ISBN 1-878352-10-5
Library of Congress Card Number: 95-69976

Exclusive distributor: McPherson & Company, Post Office Box 1126, Kingston, New York 12401.

TABLE OF CONTENTS

PREFACE AND
ACKNOWLEDGEMENTS

In 1990, when I was doing research for this book, I visited the ancient Jewish graveyard in Worms. While there, I encountered a group of young Israelis who were examining the Hebrew inscriptions on the tomb stones, some of which no doubt commemorated ancestors of these very Israelis. Then, in the oldest Jewish synagogue in Germany, which is down the road from the cemetery, I met a group of German school children whose teacher was telling them about Jewish history in medieval Germany. Spanning a period of some 1,000 years, the history of Jews in Germany forms the subject of my book. It is a subject which now, unfortunately, is a thing of the past, and it is my hope that this work will stimulate an interest in this remarkable Jewish community.

★   ★   ★

This book would not have been possible without the many histories and biographies of Jews in Germany and the writings of German Jews themselves. To all these authors, both German and

7

American, I wish to extend my gratitude. I am also indebted to my friends and colleagues who have discussed the involved issues with me and given me helpful suggestions and guidance. Finally, I am deeply indebted to the Sojourner Truth Library of the State University of New York at New Paltz and the Jewish Division of the New York Public Library, whose extensive collections in history, biography, German literature, and Judaica enabled my research. And as always I am indebted to my wife, Peggy Bowen Munsterberg, who has been a constant support and helpmate in this undertaking.

Hugo Munsterberg
January 1995

Unspoken Bequest

Ich hatte einst ein schönes Vaterland,
Der Eichenbaum
Wuchs dort so hoch, die Veilchen nickten sanft;
Es war ein Traum.

Once I had a beautiful Fatherland;
The oak tree
Grew so tall there, the violets nodded gently:
It was a dream.

HEINRICH HEINE

This book is dedicated to the memory of my grandfather,
MORITZ MÜNSTERBERG
born in Breslau in 1825,
buried in the Jewish cemetery in Danzig in 1880.

INTRODUCTION

The first Jews to reach German soil are believed to have come with the Romans, who had conquered the left bank of the Rhine and the Mosel River region during the first century before Christ.[1] Some may have been legionnaires in the Roman army, others were probably slaves, and there may have also been some Jewish merchants and physicians. While there is no documentary evidence of their arrival, many stories have come down to us about pre-Christian Jewish communities in Worms, Trier, Cologne, and Regensburg; and in the Mainz cemetery there are gravestones inscribed with Latinized forms of Jewish names.

By the fourth century after Christ, Cologne evidently had a substantial Jewish community with its own synagogue and rabbi, for there are two documents dating from 321 and 331 AD in which the Emperor Constantine I informed the city administration that Jews, who had previously been excluded from city government, were now eligible for administrative and honorary offices. As was the case for the heads of other religious groups, the leaders of the Jewish community were exempted from holding such positions.

After the conquest of this region by Germanic tribes—principally the Franks—the position of the Jews deteriorated, for there were Jewish persecutions during the sixth century. The situation did not improve until the early ninth century with Charlemagne and the rise of the Carolingian dynasty, and then the changes were remarkable. Under Charlemagne and his successors, settlements expanded as Jewish immigrants came in from Southern France and Italy, and some Jews enjoyed royal protection. In addition to Cologne and other cities on the Rhine, there was also a substantial Jewish community in Charlemagne's capital of Aachen (Aix la Chapelle).

The social position of the Jews also changed dramatically in this period: they were no longer soldiers and slaves but prominent merchants and medical doctors, and Jewish traders formed the link between the Frankish empire and the Mediterranean world. Their acumen in business and linguistics made them valuable middlemen for the Carolingian rulers in their contacts with France, Italy, and the Levant. As early as 797 AD, three years before his coronation as Holy Roman Emperor, Charlemagne included a Jewish businessman named

Isaak with an embassy to Caliph Harun al-Rashid in Baghdad, where he no doubt served as interpreter and guide. It is further recorded that Isaak was one of those who survived the long journey and brought back gifts, including an elephant, to his sovereign. Even more remarkable, the court deacon Bodo converted to Judaism in 839 and took the name Eleazar.

During the early medieval period, by and large, Jews and Christians lived at peace with each other, and Jews in the German lands continued to fare well. The Jewish people enjoyed the protection of emperors and bishops and had separate communities under the administration of their own laws. Jewish settlements flourished along the Rhine in Cologne, Mainz, Worms, and Speyer; and on the Moselle in Trier and Metz, as well as in Regensburg in Southeast Germany and in Prague in Bohemia. The earliest synagogue from this period still in existence was founded in Worms in 1014 by Jacob and Rahel ben David; its construction was completed in 1034. A contemporary document also mentions a Jewish quarter in Worms, and the oldest gravestone in the Worms Jewish cemetery is dated 1076.

On the whole, Jews formed a prosperous group, and while they stood apart from the rest of society, they were much better off economically than the mass of poverty-stricken serfs and peasants and admired for their skills as merchants, physicians, and scholars. German Jewish rabbis and Biblical scholars were highly regarded not only in Germany but throughout Europe, and were consulted about translations of the Bible and theological treatises. Indeed, the status of German Jews was second only to their coreligionists in Islamic-ruled Spain, where the Jewish communities enjoyed a period of remarkable efflorescence from the ninth through eleventh centuries.

Persecution, Expulsion, and Slaughter

At the end of the eleventh century, this tranquil state of affairs was abruptly shattered by the First Crusade. After Pope Urban II's famous exhortation to battle at the Council of Clermont, the French Jews alerted their Jewish brethren in Germany to the impending danger, but their warning was not heeded in time. Spurred by the dictum "We have travelled a long, arduous road to take possession of the Holy Sepulchre, and we will not let those who killed the Savior live among us,"[2] the crusaders swept into the Rhenish cities.

The elders of the Jewish community in Mainz dispatched a messenger asking for help to the Emperor Henry IV, who was in Italy at the time. He at once ordered his nobles and bishops in the German lands to protect their Jews but, in spite of this, there were massive persecutions, beginning in Speyer, where eleven Jews were killed in 1096. Further up the Rhine, in Worms, 800 were slain. Jews in Mainz, led by Kalonymos ben Meschullambut, put up an ultimately futile resistance to the crusaders, and were massacred or committed suicide. In Cologne, many Jews threw themselves into the Rhine, while others perished at the hands of the crusaders despite the attempts by the city's arch-bishop to protect them. Nor was there any refuge in the countryside, for those who fled to nearby villages were slaughtered by the peasants. Only those Jews who were willing to convert to Christianity were spared, but they were few in number. Most Rhenish Jews preferred torture and death to a renunciation of their ancestral faith; only in Regensberg did a sizeable number choose conversion.

The persecutions brought about by the First Crusade took place over a period of only three months, during which time an estimated 12,000 Jews lost their lives. That number may seem small compared to the millions exterminated during the twentieth-century Holocaust, but in proportion to the size of the Jewish population in Germany at that time, it is immense. It must be remembered, however, that the crusaders slaughtered people indiscriminately as they advanced through East-ern Europe and the Near East, and that local rulers and even bishops did not hesitate to kill rebellious Chris-tians as well.

When Henry IV returned from Italy in 1097, he permitted the Jews who had been forcibly converted to return to Judaism and ordered an investigation into the actions of the archbishop of Mainz, who was suspected of having appropriated the property of the Jews in his realm. There can be no doubt that envy of Jewish wealth and financial indebtedness to Jews played im-portant roles in the Jewish persecutions.

The Second Crusade, five decades later, brought far less havoc to Jews, as Bernard of Clairvaux, the French clergyman who had persuaded Emperor Conrad III to undertake it, warned against excesses, and both the emperor and the bishops offered their protection to the Jewish communities.

The Third Crusade, from 1189 to 1192, also resulted in little damage to Jews, as Emperor Frederick I had ordered that anyone who murdered a Jew should be executed, and that anyone who injured a Jew would have his arms cut off. Nevertheless, crusaders persecuted some Jews in the Rhenish cities of Neuss, Boppard, and Speyer.

The Crusades continued through the thirteenth century, and the position of the Jews continued to deteriorate, not only in Germany but across Europe. A movement to restrict the activities of Jews, especially their financial dealings, started with the Fourth Lateran Council of 1215 and was confirmed by the councils in Fritzlar and Breslau in 1259 and 1267. Strict usury regulations were aimed at the interest charged on loans made by Jews. A decree that Jews could not live next to Christians led to the formation of the Ghetto; and Jews were required to wear special dress—a funnel hat, and a yellow ring on their clothes. Accusations of ritual murder and desecration of Christian symbols became commonplace, and despite the emperor's and the pope's rejection of these changes, they led to Jewish persecutions in the Rhineland and Bavaria during the second half of the thirteenth century. With the advent of the

Black Death in 1348, the persecutions increased, because it was said that Jews had caused the plague by poisoning the water in the wells.

Throughout Europe, Jews were being forced out of their homelands. They were expelled from England in 1290 and from France in 1392. Finally, after one of the bloodiest periods of the Spanish Inquisition, which saw the killing of an estimated 100,000 Jews and the forced conversions of many others, the inquisitor-general, Torquemada, ordered the expulsion of all Jews from Spain. Portugal followed suit in 1497.

Until the twentieth-century Holocaust, the Torquemada Inquisition was the most horrible catastrophe Jews ever suffered. It brought to a brutal end the largest and most remarkable Jewish community in Europe, for while the Moslem rulers of Spain had given their Jewish subjects favor and protection, the new rulers of Aragon and Castille, Ferdinand and Isabella, gave them death, conversion, or exile.

Although the official rationale for these persecutions was that the Jews not only rejected the Christian Savior but were the descendents of the people who had crucified him, there can be no doubt that economic motives were also prominent. As a contemporary chronicle put it, "Do you want to know what brought the Jews their misfortune? It was the greed of the Christians." Beginning with the emperors themselves, who regarded Jews as imperial servants and levied a heavy tribute for protection, everyone in authority—bishops, local rulers, and even city officials—demanded large payments and otherwise made life for the Jewish communities very difficult. As as result, many Jews fled east, especially to Poland, where the king welcomed them. There was a great need for artisans and merchants in Poland, as the population consisted largely of nobles and peasants.

Once the Jews were gone from Germany, the rulers began to miss the revenue they had extracted from them, so some Jews were readmitted to the cities. The first to take them back were Speyer and Worms, which had had very old Jewish settlements; Mainz, Basel, Strasbourg, and Cologne followed in short order. For the most part, however, Jews were given permission to stay only for a limited number of years and, as a result, the once flourishing Jewish communities of Germany never regained the prominence and wealth they had enjoyed in the early medieval period.

Throughout these constant persecutions, however, Jewish communities did survive in German lands, in large part because medieval Germany was divided into hundreds of small states, each under its own jurisdiction. Thus the Jews who were expelled from Cologne in 1424 could easily move across the Rhine to Deutz, or south to Bonn, or north to Neuss. Those expelled from Hamburg could settle in Altona, which belonged to the Danes, and Jews who were no longer tolerated in Nuremberg were welcomed in neighboring Fürth, which had an old Jewish community that in the twentieth century would produce such outstanding figures as Jacob Wasserman and Henry Kissinger. At this time,

Frankfurt had the largest Jewish community, about 5,000 altogether, but they were restricted to the Judengasse, a ghetto which still existed as late as the eighteenth century.

The Late Renaissance and the Enlightenment

During the seventeenth and eighteenth century, the most important new development for Jews in Germany was the emergence of the so-called court Jews. These were men who worked as financial advisors to the local rulers and noble families, and they often wielded considerable power. As both the secular and spiritual rulers of Germany were in constant need of money to finance their splendid courts and extravagant lives, they frequently borrowed money from such Jewish financiers as Meyer zu Goldstein in Cologne and Aaron Beer in Frankfurt. The most powerful and notorious of court Jews was Joseph Süss Oppenheimer, who was given the title of financial counselor to the ruler of Würtemberg in the southwest. Although he had a brilliant career and for many years successfully managed the finances of his sovereign, he came to a bitter end after the death of his patron in 1738, for he was executed on the grounds that he had exploited the common people.

At this time the majority of German Jews lived in simple circumstances and faced an uncertain life in a society that barely tolerated them. Prevented by law from owning land and excluded from many professions, they were forced into trade and moneylending, many of them working as itinerant peddlers whose meager livings were made by selling cheap merchandise in rural villages. But some Jewish merchants fared better. Of the growing number of those whose specialty was textiles, for example, some controlled textile factories and trading firms. By the late seventeenth century, Jewish merchants were becoming established in German trade. In 1675, some 400 to 600 Jewish merchants participated in the great Leipzig trade fair, and by 1700, no fewer than 1200 took part in it. Another indication of the growing importance of the Jewish merchants to Germany was the overture that Frederick William the Great Elector of Brandenburg (the future Prussia), made to well-to-do Jews in 1671, inviting them to settle in Berlin under favorable conditions.

A fascinating account of the life of one of these prosperous middle-class Jewish merchant families is the memoir of a Jewish woman, Glückel von Hameln. Written in 1690, it gives a vivid picture of her life and the society in which she lived. Von Hameln wrote in Yiddish, the lingua franca of the Jewish community, but her memoir was widely read and has been translated into both German and English.[3] Although she and her family were not part of the larger German society, she was keenly observant, and seems to have enjoyed a rich and fulfilling life as a member of a large Jewish family with many international ties.

The Enlightenment and the French Revolution brought about a fundamental change in the position of all Jews in Germany. Not all German states gave their Jewish subjects equal rights from one day to next, but because of the more rational and liberal ideas of the period, Jews began to be regarded not as a separate and unequal religious community but first as fellow men and ultimately as fellow citizens. One of the first signs of the new age in Germany was the publication in 1781 of the Prussian military counselor Friedrich Wilhelm von Dohm's *On the Civil Improvement of the Jews.* Another milestone was the celebrated 1779 play *Nathan der Weise* ("Nathan the Wise") by the famous philosopher and literary critic Gotthold Ephraim Lessing, the first major work in which the hero is a Jew. Both these authors were profoundly influenced by the well-known philosopher Moses Mendelssohn, a friend of Immanuel Kant and a leading figure in the intellectual and cultural life of Berlin.

Others who welcomed Jews as fellow citizens were Wilhelm von Humboldt (1767-1835), the Prussian statesman and minister of education, and Karl August von Hardenberg (1750-1822), who, as state chancellor of Prussia, was responsible for the legislation that gave Jews the rights of citizenship. Jews now had to take German family names and all their official documents had to be in the German language. This development was welcomed by the entire Jewish community. Only the extreme Orthodox had reservations about the price that Jews would have to pay for full emancipation, for liberal reformers and humanists like Humboldt, while welcoming the Jews into German society, expected them to assimilate completely and assumed that in due time they would give up the faith of their ancestors.

Jews in Nineteenth-Century Germany

In 1815, with the Congress of Vienna and the redrawing of the map of Europe, the several German states united loosely into the German Confederation, thus sowing the first seeds of German national identity. This, and to a larger extent the Romantic movement which was reaching its peak at the time, resulted in a certain retrogression of the German attitude toward Jews. Citizenship rights were restricted in some states and Jews were expelled from some cities, Bremen and Lübeck among them. Voices hostile to full Jewish participation in German political and cultural life could be heard. In Berlin, for example, the historian Fredrich Rühs wrote a book in which he opposed giving Jews rights equal to those of Christians and further asserted that it would be best if Jews as a people would cease to exist. Even more radical was the Heidelberg philosopher Jacob Fries, whose advocacy for expelling Jews from villages and restricting their economic activity harkened back to medieval times. Despite these voices of hatred, however, both assimilation and civil and cultural emancipation moved forward, and by the middle of the nineteenth century Jews enjoyed most of the rights of citizenship.

The culmination of these liberal and democratic tendencies of the nineteenth century came in 1848, when popular revolution broke out not only in Paris, but throughout Germany as well. Meeting in St. Paul's Church in Frankfurt, delegates of the various political parties convened a national assembly, the Frankfurt Parliament, which passed sweeping legislation that included equal rights for Jews. How greatly the status of German Jews had changed is underscored by the fact that four of the deputies to the national assembly were Jews, one of whom, Gabriel Riesner, was elected vice president of the Parliament. Another seventeen delegates were Jews who had converted to Christianity and men of Jewish descent, including Eduard Simson, who was elected president of the assembly.[4]

The revolutions in Germany were soon defeated, and the Frankfurt Parliament disbanded, bringing Jews some reverses, but the movement toward greater equality could not be stopped. With the rise of Bismark and the establishment of the German Empire in 1871, Jewish emancipation became complete. Jews could now move freely, own land, enter any profession, attend universities and teach in them, and occupy public office. Although there were still some restrictions—especially in regard to military commissions and high government office, Jews now became prominent in politics. Ludwig Bamberger was a leading Liberal Party member of parliament, and Eduard Lasker founded the National Liberal Party.

The years of the German Empire, 1871 to 1918, were a golden age for German Jews. Freed from all but a few restrictions, they not only established themselves in German society but regarded themselves as truly German, identifying with the humanistic tradition of Lessing, Goethe, and Schiller. Most now belonged to the middle class, the chief exception being the Polish Jews of the eastern provinces who were looked down upon even by German Jews. They also tended to become more and more urban, leaving the villages and small towns for the big cities, especially Berlin and Frankfurt, and they attended universities in ever increasing numbers. In fact, although they comprised only one percent of the general German population, ten percent of the university population was Jewish.

Large numbers of Jews were now entering medicine, the sciences, and law. Others were journalists and critics, many playing prominent roles in newspaper, magazine, and book publishing. In the arts, German Jews became particularly influential in music, the theatre, and, somewhat later, the film industry. Even more important was their position in business. Gerson Bleichröder served as Chancellor Bismark's banker and financial advisor; Emil Rathenau founded the great electrical combine AEG, which was one of the largest industrial enterprises in Germany; Albert Ballin, founder of the greatest German shipping line, became a friend and consultant of Emperor William II. As the German-born American historian Fritz Stern said, "In the last century German Jews managed as great a leap forward as any minority has ever achieved in European history."[5]

26

No doubt it seemed to the Jews like a slow and uneven progress, with many rejections and disappointments, but viewed from the long range, the change in their position was quite extraordinary. A repressed minority speaking a foreign tongue and living in communities that were completely separate from German society had become part of the German nation, enjoying the same rights and opportunities as their Christian fellow citizens. While there were many conversions and, after the institution of civil marriage in 1875, many "mixed" marriages, the great majority of the German Jews remained faithful to Judaism, describing themselves as German citizens of the Jewish faith (which was also the name of their largest organization at that time).

Although the process of Jewish assimilation into the mainstream of German life continued throughout the nineteenth century, it did encounter two main obstacles. One came from Jews themselves, particularly Orthodox Jews, who feared they would lose their religious and cultural identity. In 1872, a seminary for Orthodox rabbis was founded in Berlin; earlier, Abraham Geiger had established the School for the Science of Judaism. At the end of the century, Theodor Herzl founded the Zionist movement, to which Heinrich Graetz, in his eleven-volume historical work on the Jews, referred as a nation rather than a religious community.[6]

There were also voices raised among the Germans themselves, some of whom no longer welcomed assimilation because they regarded Jews as belonging to an alien and inferior Semitic race: even if Jews became Christian, they could never be truly German. Some of these naysayers, such as Hermann Ahlwardt and Wilhelm Marr, were merely vicious demagogues, but others were influential figures in German society. The court preacher Adolf Stöcker, for example, founded an anti-Semitic party which was able to elect sixteen members to the parliament. And the famous historian Heinrich Treitschke said, "The Jews are our misfortune," while the philosopher Eugen Dühring rejected the Jewish race as parasitic. Worst of all was Richard Wagner, who saw Jews as the enemy of mankind.

During World War I, German Jews proved their German patriotism by volunteering for armed service and performing honorably in the field. When William II declared that there were no longer people of different parties or social classes but only Germans, Jews felt that he had also spoken for them. With the exception of a few convinced pacifists such as Albert Einstein, and socialists like Rosa Luxemburg who regarded the conflict as war between imperial rulers and not peoples, the German Jews joined in the war for Kaiser and Fatherland. More than 100,000 Jews served in the armed forces, of whom 12,000 were killed and no fewer than 30,000 decorated with the Iron Cross. One Jewish soldier even received the Pour le Mérite, the highest award given by the German army.

The Jewish contribution to the war effort was by no means restricted to service in the armed forces. Walter Rathenau, the head of AEG, developed a plan for the war economy and became a virtual tsar of the war industry. Fritz Haber, the chemist and head of the Kaiser Wilhelm Institute, invented a process of creating nitrate from air, which freed Germany from depending upon imported nitrate for its munitions industry. Other Jews served in the medical branch of the military forces or as scientific experts. The work of all these men was dedicated to the cause of German victory. In 1918, when General Ludendorf sued for peace, it was a Jew, Walter Rathenau, who called for a mass uprising to continue the war, while Albert Ballin, the Jewish shipping magnat, took his own life in despair over Germany's defeat.

Into the Holocaust and Aftermath

With the end of the German Empire and the establishment of the Weimar Republic, the last restrictions on Jews were removed. Walter Rathenau became foreign minister, the highest position any German Jew was ever to attain; Hugo Preuss was largely responsible for writing the Weimar constitution, and no fewer than three ministerial offices in the Republic were occupied by men who were either Jews or of Jewish origin. In Berlin, much of the cultural life was in Jewish hands: such figures as Max Reinhardt and Leopold Jessner were prominent in the theatre; Bruno Walter and Otto Klemperer were the foremost symphonic conductors; and Ullstein and Mosse were the nation's most influential newspaper publishers. By and large, German Jews enthusiastically supported the new state, and were especially active in the liberal Democratic Party. But during the 1920s, anti-Semites were gaining ground. They blamed the Jews for the defeat in the war, accusing them of having enriched themselves during the years of inflation and pointing out that many radicals, such as Rosa Luxemburg, had been Jews. Claiming that the Weimar Republic was the *"Juden Republik,"* members of the far right assassinated the Jewish foreign minister, Walter Rathenau. Adolf Hitler, who had founded the National Socialist German Workers Party in 1919 and attempted a putsch in 1923, was merely one of many right-wing extremists who agitated both against the Treaty of Versailles and the Jews, who in their eyes had become far too powerful and influential. Anti-Semitism, which had always existed, became more blatant, especially after 1929 when economic misery and political chaos enveloped Germany.

Nevertheless, these small anti-Semitic parties had only a marginal role in the political life of the country during the 1920s, and indeed most Germans considered them part of a lunatic fringe. During these years, the largest parties in the Reichstag were the Social Democrats, the Catholic Centrum Party, and the Communist Party, all of whom fully accepted their Jewish fellow citizens. Even the conservative German National Party was never overtly anti-Semitic. However, all of this changed when the National Socialist Party (Nazi Party) won a great election victory in 1930 and became the second largest party in the German parliament.

In 1933, having been named chancellor by the aged President Hindenburg, Hitler began to consolidate his power, outlawing all but the Nazi Party and "coordinating" every aspect of life in Germany. By the following year, Hindenburg was dead, the Third Reich was born, and Hitler was both chancellor and president as *führer*. Just how important a role anti-Semitism played in Hitler's rise to power has been the subject of intensive scrutiny and debate by both German and American social scientists. Their conclusions suggest that it was a relatively minor factor, accounting for no more than ten percent of the vote, a conclusion that is reinforced by the fact that for more than a decade the anti-Semitic parties did not attract many followers in Germany. It was only after the Great Depression had ruined large sections of the middle class and left six million unemployed that the voters turned to the radical parties of both the right and the left. The other factor, which no doubt accounted for Hitler's great appeal, was his strident nationalism and his promise to lead the German people back to greatness and power. In Hitler's mind, this goal was probably his overriding concern, with economic recovery and the destruction of Jews subordinate to it.

Although Hitler had made his virulent anti-Semitism clear in his book *Mein Kamph*, and the curtailment of Jewish influence had always been a major point in the Nazi party program, the German Jewish community did not immediately appreciate the danger it was in.

31

Thinking of themselves as good Germans, Jews simply could not believe that Hitler fully meant what he said. They thought that while pogroms might take place in tsarist Russia, they certainly could not occur in their *Vaterland*. In the first year of the new regime, only 25,000 out of more than 500,000 Jews fled from Germany, most of them left wing radicals whose lives were in danger. Even after the 1935 Nuremberg racial laws had been passed and the restrictions on Jewish activities had become more oppressive, relatively few German Jews emigrated. No doubt many were reluctant to start life over again in a foreign land; others did not wish to lose all their possessions, and still others found it difficult to get the proper papers to enter other countries. It was not until Kristallnacht, in November 1938, when synagogues were set on fire, Jewish places of business destroyed, and Jews arrested en masse, that German Jews saw the peril they were in. Only then did they recognize that Hitler's ultimate intent was to expel or to exterminate them, and those who had not already left now tried frantically to flee Germany before it was too late.

It is estimated that of the half-million Jews who were living in Germany when Hitler came to power, some 300,000 escaped and 200,000 ended in the gas ovens, committed suicide, or died of disease or starvation. Most of those who got out of Germany came to the United States, sometimes by a circuitous route which took them first to places as far afield as Cuba and Shanghai. Others, especially Zionists, went to Palestine to help build a Jewish state, and still others emigrated to Great Britain, France, Canada, Australia, South Africa, and South America. After the "Final Solution" of 1941 had been implemented, only a few thousand Jews remained in Germany. Some were in hiding, others had false papers, but most of those who survived within Germany were married to non-Jewish spouses which gave them the possibility, if not the guarantee, of protection. By the end of World War II, the thousand-year-old Jewish community in Germany had come to an end; almost all German Jews had either fled or been murdered by the Nazis.

Today only small Jewish communities exist in the large German cities, particularly in Berlin and Frankfurt. These are comprised of a total of perhaps 30,000 survivors and returnees, including some Polish, Russian, and other East European Jews who settled in Germany after the war.

NOTES

[1] G. Ristov, *Zur Frühgeschichte der Rheinischen Juden in Monumenta Judaica* (Cologne: 1963), 33.

[2] H.G. Adler, *Die Juden in Deutschland* (Munich: 1960), 23 (author's translation).

[3] *Denkwürdigkeiten der Glückel von Hameln* (Berlin: 1913); *The Memoirs of Glückel of Hameln* (New York: Harper, 1932).

[4] Alder, 76.

[5] F. Stern, *Gold and Iron* (New York: Vintage, 1979, c1977), xxiii.

[6] Heinrich Graetz, *A History of the Jews* (1853-75), trans. by Bella Lowy (Philadelphia: Jewish Publication Society of America, 1891-98).

MOSES MENDELSSOHN

I: PHILOSOPHY

It was in the field of philosophy that German Jews made their first significant contribution to German culture. This is not surprising, for the Jews of Germany were known for their learning and scholarship as early as the medieval period. Then, their studies were principally in the Hebrew language and dealt with the Torah and its commentaries, intellectual activities that disciplined their minds and sharpened their reasoning and debating skills. Rabbinical students from all over Europe came to Germany to sit at the feet of famous German Jewish teachers in order to be introduced to traditional Jewish learning. Although such instruction was restricted to the Jewish community, it is reported that even medieval Christian biblical scholars sometimes turned to their Jewish colleagues for help in interpreting obscure passages of the Old Testament. However, in the eighteenth century with the coming of the Enlightenment, all this changed as Jewish scholars began to play significant roles in the non-Jewish intellectual life of Germany as well. By the nineteenth century, Jews were appointed to university positions for the first time, and by the twentieth century, several of the leading philosophers in Germany were either Jews or men of Jewish origin.

Among these men, the most important was Edmund Husserl (born in Prossnitz, 1859, died in Freiburg, 1938). He became a professor of philosophy first in Göttingen, one of Germany's oldest and most prestigious universities, and later taught at Freiburg University. Until his discharge in 1933, when the Nazis came to power, he had a brilliant academic career and was much esteemed. He is celebrated today as the founder of phenomenology, which attempts to put philosophy on a scientific basis by the descriptive study of consciousness in relationship to objects. His analysis of the role of sense perception between the subjective ego and the reality of the object had a great influence on many modern philosophers, notably Martin Heidegger, who had been one of his students, and Jean Paul Sartre. Husserl's main work was *Logical Inquiries* of 1900, but his writings were voluminous and fifty thousand pages of his notes are still being worked on at the Husserl Archives in Louvain and Cologne.

An almost exact contemporary of Husserl's was Georg Simmel (born in Berlin, 1858, died in Strasbourg, 1918). He taught at Berlin University, and, during the last years of his life, in Strasbourg. In Berlin, one of his students was the Spanish-born American philosopher and poet George Santayana. Simmel was famous for his brilliant lectures and his extensive writings which dealt with a broad range of subjects. Today, he is probably best known as one of the founders of sociology and author of *The Philosophy of Money*. In addition to his sociological and philosophical writings, he also wrote books on Kant, Goethe, Schopenhauer, and Nietzsche.

Somewhat older was Hermann Cohen (born in Coswig, 1842, died in Marburg, 1918). Early in his life, Cohen had studied to become a rabbi, but he abandoned his theological studies for philosophy. As a professor of philosophy at Marburg University, he became the leading figure in the Marburg School of neo-Kantian thought, which played a significant role in German and European philosophy in the early twentieth century. Unlike Husserl and Simmel, who had not concerned themselves with the Jewish tradition, Cohen was deeply attached to his ancestral religion, especially in his later years. He saw Judaism as a religion of reason and tried to reconcile its teachings with rational philosophy. For him, ethics, law, and moral behavior were the essence of religion, rather than revealed religion, mysticism, and pietism, which he rejected. Cohen became known for his commentaries on the writings of Immanuel Kant.

Another quite different thinker was Ernst Bloch (born in Ludwigshafen, 1885, died in Tübingen, 1977). A utopian Marxist, his thought was far removed from

Judaism as well as traditional philosophy. Bloch's first major work was on the sixteenth-century Anabaptist social revolutionary Thomas Münzer, but he is best known for *The Philosophy of Hope*, written between 1938 and 1947 and published in the 1950s. Forced to flee his native country during the Hitler era, he spent ten years in the United States. After the war, he returned to a partioned Germany, first to East Germany, where he taught in Leipzig. Later, he moved to West Germany and taught at Tübingen, south of Stuttgart, where he enjoyed his most successful period, with the young radical students of the late 1960s hailing him as the boldest and most relevant thinker of his generation.

By far the most famous German Jewish philosopher and one of the most influential of all German Jews was Moses Mendelssohn, who lived from 1729 to 1786. Although his philosophical writings are not much read today, during his lifetime and into the nineteenth and twentieth centuries he was highly regarded not only in his native Germany but throughout Europe. In 1863, his collected writings were published in seven volumes and a more complete edition of all his works was prepared in the twentieth century. His two most famous books, *Phaedon* (1767) and *Jerusalem* (1783), have been reprinted in English as recently as 1973 and 1969, respectively, and his letters have been edited in several different editions. An extensive literature on his life and work exists in both German and English.

Of the German biographies, Meyer Kayserling's *Moses*

Mendelssohn, Sein Leben und seine Werke, which was first published in 1862 and came out in a revised edition in 1888, is the most comprehensive. In 1929, on the occasion of the two hundredth anniversary of Mendelssohn's birth, a major study of his life and works written by various scholars was published in Berlin. There are also important biographies in English, notably Hermann Walter's *Moses Mendelssohn, Critic and Philosopher* (1930) and Alexander Altmann's *Moses Mendelssohn, A Biographical Study* (1973). A monument in the form of a bust of Mendelssohn was erected in his native city of Dessau in 1978, demonstrating that his example and contributions to German culture are still appreciated, and there is an extensive Mendelssohn Archive in Berlin.

Moses Mendelssohn represents a link between worlds of the early Jewish Ghetto and the Age of Enlightenment. Born in the well-established Jewish community in Dessau, the young Mendelssohn grew up in a Yiddish-speaking environment in which the Talmudic learning and Hebrew studies flourished. His father, Mendel Heymann, was a simple man, the custodian at the local synagogue and a scribe who made copies of the Torah. His mother came from a prominent German Jewish family whose ancestors had been leading Jewish scholars. Although his body was somewhat hunchbacked, young Moses' mind was brilliant, and it is said that at the age of six he began to study Hebrew texts; as a child he already showed great intellectual promise.

While Mendelssohn's relationship to his parents does

not seem to have been especially close, he was quite attached to the chief rabbi of Dessau, David Fränkel, who became his adoptive father and spiritual mentor. Under Fränkel's tutelage, the young boy was introduced to Jewish learning. Early on he developed a great fondness for the Bible, which in later years he translated into German, but the main emphasis of his study was on the Talmud. It was during this period that he discovered the great Jewish philosophers of the medieval period, notably Moses Maimonides who had lived during the second half of the twelfth century. A product of the illustrious Jewish community of Moslem Spain, Maimonides was known for his religious tolerance and his interest in Greek philosophy. His most famous work, which has influenced both Jewish and Christian thought, is *Guide for the Perplexed*. Originally written in Arabic around 1190, it was translated into Hebrew, Latin, and all modern Western languages.

In 1743, David Fränkel was chief rabbi of Berlin, and Mendelssohn—or Moses Dessau as he then called himself—followed him there. He was thirteen years old. At that time, Berlin had a Jewish community of about two thousand people and was a great center of Jewish learning. Most Jews lived near the Spree River, where there was a splendid synagogue and where the wealthiest and most prominent Jew, Veitel Heine Ephraim, had built a palace. The ruler of Prussia was then Frederick the Great, an enlightened monarch who was a friend of Voltaire and tolerated Jews—especially those who could contribute to the Prussian economy.

The atmosphere of Berlin proved stimulating to the young Moses. Not only did he study under distinguished scholars of Hebrew and the Talmud, but for the first time he encountered thinkers of the Enlightenment, such as the Marquis d'Argens, a protogé of the king and a member of the Royal Academy. Mendelssohn also studied language. He had grown up speaking only Yiddish and Hebrew but now he was taught Latin and introduced to Greek by Aaron Soloman Gumpertz, who was only six years his elder and who came from an old and distinguished Jewish family. He also studied French and English on his own in order to read the rationalist philosophers and, even more important for his later development, now became a master of the German language. Indeed, he not only wrote most of his books in German, but he became an outstanding stylist in the German language as well.

But while Mendelssohn feasted on the richness of Berlin's intellectual life, he lived a mere hand-to-mouth existence. His family were poor and could spare little or nothing to send him to the university, so his teenage years in Berlin were hard ones. That changed in 1750, when he was twenty-one, and was invited into the household of Isaac Bernard, a prosperous silk manufacturer, as the private tutor of the Bernard children. When the children grew up, Mendelssohn joined the Bernard silk business and, after Isaac's death, took over the factory. Although the business took much of his attention, it provided a secure financial base for him and his family, and it also left him enough free time to pursue his interests in philosophy.

During the early 1750s, Mendelssohn became acquainted with the great tradition of European philosophy about which he had previously known nothing. The thinkers he admired most were the English philosopher John Locke and the German philosophers Gottfried Wilhelm Leibniz and Christian Freihert von Wolff. Locke's essays, *Concerning Human Understanding* (1690), which he first read in Latin, made a profound impression on him, as did the writings of Leibniz. But it was probably von Wolff, now forgotten but at that time a well-known philosopher, whose writings influenced him the most. Wolff's *Vernünftige Gedanken* ("Rational Thoughts" [1719]), which deals in a rational manner with metaphysics and ethics, opened up a whole new world for Mendelssohn. A Jewish philosopher of Holland and contemporary of Wolff, Leibniz, and Locke whom he studied diligently was Benedict (Baruch) Spinoza; but although Mendelssohn admired Spinoza greatly, he never followed him in his rejection of traditional Judaism.

Mendelssohn's first philosophical work was a fragment entitled *Chance Happenings*, which was written in 1753 and found in his notebooks after his death. The following year, when Mendelssohn celebrated his twenty-fifth birthday, he met Gotthold Lessing and Friedrich Nicolai, who were to become his closest friends and have a deep influence on his intellectual development. A philosopher, literary critic, and dramatist, Lessing was the greatest German writer before Goethe. Before he met Mendelssohn, he had already written the drama *Die Juden* (1749), in which Jews were portrayed in a favorable light for the first time in German literature. He wrote his most celebrated drama *Nathan der Weise*, in 1779. Its hero is a thinly disguised Moses Mendelssohn, his friend then for twenty-five years. Nicolai was also a writer, as well as an editor and publisher, and in that capacity printed Mendelssohn's early works.

Both Lessing and Nicolai belonged to Berlin's intellectual elite, and they introduced Mendelssohn to a world which, as a Jew and a man without any formal academic training, he could otherwise not have entered. But despite his close friendship with these men, Mendelssohn never severed his relationship with Berlin's Jewish community. He attended services at the Berlin synagogue throughout his life and translated Rabbi Fränkel's sermons into German. Even more significant, in 1758, he and a friend edited a Hebrew weekly called *Kohelet Mussar* ("Preacher of Morals"). The aim of the journal was to strengthen the morals of Jewish youth and to cultivate the love of Hebrew, but this venture was short-lived, for the magazine folded after only two issues.

In the 1760s, Mendelssohn emerged as one of the leading thinkers in Germany. In 1761 he published his *Philosophische Schriften* ("Philosophical Notes"), which established his reputation as a philosopher, and in 1763 he won the first prize in a competition sponsored by the Berlin Academy for the best philosophical essay, a competition in which Kant was the runner-up. In 1767, he published his *Phaedon, or On the Immortality of the Soul*, which created a sensation and remains one of his best known works. With it he became a celebrity not only in Germany but throughout Europe. The book quickly sold out, went through many more printings, and was translated into Dutch, French, Italian, Danish, Russian, English, and Hebrew.

The title of the English edition is *Phaedon or the Death of Socrates by Moses Mendelssohn, A Jew, Late of Berlin*. The first part of the work is devoted to the life and character of Socrates, but the bulk of the book consists of a retelling of the Socratic dialogues in the spirit of the Enlightenment. As Alexander Altmann put it in his excellent book on Mendelssohn, by projecting his own ideas upon Socrates, Mendelssohn made his hero not only into a Leibnizian but also into a Mendelssohn. Thus his description of the character of Socrates may be read profitably as a guide to the understanding of Mendelssohn himself. Although he used the form of Socratic dialogue, Mendelssohn employed the language and the arguments of the Enlightenment, thereby bringing the philosophical ideas closer to those of his contemporaries.[1]

Mendelssohn was both a man of the Enlightenment, with all this entailed concerning rationalism and humanism, and a pious Jew who attended the synagogue, observed the dietary laws, and celebrated the Jewish holidays. In 1771, he was elected to the Berlin Academy of Science, a rare honor, especially for a Jew, but it was an honor to which Frederick the Great did not consent. However, the king did invite Mendelssohn to his palace in Potsdam, because the Saxon minister wished to meet the celebrated philosopher. As a scholar, Mendelssohn enjoyed the friendship of such leading intellectuals as Kant, Lessing, and the famous Orientalist Michaelis. At the same time, he referred to himself as a member of the Jewish nation and was elected honorary leader of the Jewish community of Berlin. He also continued his theological studies and translated the Psalms and the Pentateuch into German.

Mendelssohn's interpretation of Judaism helped to make his dual allegiance to his religion and philosophy easier. Unlike the exponents of traditional Orthodoxy, he rejected revelation as well as mysticism, and understood Jewish religion as being based largely on reason and morality. As he said in a letter to his friend Elkan Herz:

> Blessed be the Lord who gave us the Tora of Truth. We have no principles that are contrary to, or above, reason. Thank God, we add to natural religion nothing except commandments, statutes, and religious ordinances. As for the principles and fundamental tenets of our religion, they are based on reason and agree in every respect and without any contradiction or conflict whatever with the results of inquiry and true speculation.[2]

As Socrates had, he acknowledged the greatness and moral perfection of Christ, but he rejected the claim of divinity for Jesus. And when the Swiss theologian Johann Kasper Lavater tried to convert Mendelssohn by challenging him to prove that Judaism was superior to

45

Christianity, he left no doubt that he thought the faith of his fathers was superior to the pious emotionalism of Lavater's followers.

The important position that Mendelssohn occupied not only in Berlin but throughout Germany and other European countries is best illustrated by his interventions in Jewish affairs. In 1769, for instance, the Jewish community in Altona, at that time under Danish rule, turned to Mendelssohn when charges were leveled against it; and in 1772 the Jews of Schwerin also asked him for help. In both cases, his advice was heeded and the problems were solved. Even more impressive was his intervention when the tiny Jewish community in Switzerland was threatened with oppression in 1775 and appealed to him for help. He turned to his friend Lavater, and, as a result, a favorable solution to the trouble was worked out. Perhaps the most dramatic example of his influence came about in Dresden, where Jews were under the threat of exile if they would not pay an excessive tax levied by the government. They appealed to Mendelssohn, who, through his connections in the Saxon court and his reputation in official circles, was able to persuade government officials to rescind the new law, a remarkable proof of the respect he commanded not only in his own Prussia but across Germany.

Yet, despite the universal esteem which Mendelssohn enjoyed, his attempt to reconcile traditional Judaism with rationalistic philosophy met with criticism from both conservatives and liberals. To begin with, his translation of the five books of Moses aroused the opposition of the Orthodox rabbis, who feared that this would not only lead to a neglect of Hebrew, but would also encourage young Jews to study German literature and culture instead of the Torah and the Talmud. From the other side, his philosophical friends saw no reason why a man who had reduced the Jewish religion to a rational and moral one should not embrace a liberal version of Christianity or become a deist, as many of them had done.

In 1783, in response to these critics, Mendelssohn published his second major work, *Jerusalem,* the only one of his books which is still widely read today. Divided into two parts, the first discusses the relationship between the state and religion, in which the philosopher advocates religious tolerance and a clear separation between secular power and religious life. In the second part, he gives his definition of Judaism, which he saw as essentially in harmony with reason:

> To sum it up in one sentence: I believe Judaism knows nothing of a *revealed religion* in the sense in which Christians define this term. The Israelites possess a *divine legislation*—laws, commandments, statutes, rules of conduct, instruction in God's will and in what they are to do to attain temporal and eternal salvation. Moses, in a miraculous and supernatural way, revealed to them these laws and commandments, but not dogmas, propositions concerning salvation, or self-evident principles of reason. These the Lord reveals to us as well as to all other men at times through nature and events but never through the spoken or written word.[3]

47

Mendelssohn's last major book was his *Morgenstunden* ("Morning Hours"), published in 1785 when he was fifty-six years old, one year before his death. Some critics have called it his most profound work, but it has few readers today. In it, he argues for the exisitence of God, presenting his case step by step in seventeen lectures. It is Mendelssohn's most systematic treatise, and, once again, he presents his rationalist outlook, contrasting it to materialism on the one hand and emotional religiousity on the other. Kant, who had emerged as Germany's leading philosopher after the publication of his *Critique of Pure Reason* in 1781, disagreed with much of Mendelssohn's argument, but he praised *Morgenstunden* as the perfect embodiment of Enlightenment metaphysics. In a letter to Professor Christian Gottfried Schültz, he said, "Although the work of the worthy Mendelssohn is to be considered in the main as a masterpiece of the self-deception of our reason...it is nevertheless an excellent work."[4]

Mendelssohn died on January 4, 1786, the same year as Frederick the Great, king of Prussia. His loss was felt keenly by the Jewish community in Berlin as well as by intellectuals throughout Germany. Jewish shops and offices in Berlin were closed until after his funeral. His coffin was borne by his friends, and many of Germany's most prominent men, Jewish and gentile, were there to pay him tribute. A Hebrew dirge, written for the occasion by his friend Hartwig Wessely, praised his achievements and celebrated his immortality. Simon Hochheimer, in a verse composed in both Hebrew and German, praised him as "Moses, a man of God, the prince of the House of Jacob, the shepard of Israel, the mighty man, leader, spokesman, and protector of his people."[5] The sentiments of his Christian friends were best expressed by Karl Ramler, who called him the embodiment of wisdom and virtue and wrote an epitaph for Mendelssohn's memorial bust which reads, *Moses Mendelssohn, wise like Socrates; loyal to the faith of his fathers; like him he taught immortality; and he immortalized himself like him.*[6]

NOTES

[1] Alexander Altmann, M*oses Mendelssohn, A Biographical Study* (Alabama University Press, 1973), 149-50.

[2] Altmann, 249.

[3] Moses Mendelssohn, *Jerusalem, and other Jewish Writings*, trans. A. Jospe (New York: Shocken, 1969), 61.

[4] Altmann, 284.

[5] Altmann, 741.

[6] See also: Alexander Altmann, *Essays in Jewish Intellectual History* (Hanover, N.H.: Published for Brandeis University Press by University Press of New England, 1981); and Moses Mendelssohn, *Love Letters to His Bride* (Annandale-on-Hudson, N.Y.: Begos & Rosenberg, c1991).

MARTIN BUBER

II: RELIGIOUS THOUGHT

The central force in Jewish life has always been its religion. In fact, it could well be said that without it the Jews would never have survived as a distinct people during the centuries of the diaspora when they were scattered throughout the world. Because religious study formed an essential part of Jewish life, the rabbis assumed an important role in Jewish society.

In the medieval period, one of the great centers of Jewish religious scholarship was in the Rhineland, at the Talmudic yeshiva in Mainz founded by the early eleventh-century rabbi Gershom ben Judah. Known as the Light of Exile, his interpretations and announcements had the force of law among Jews in Germany, France, and Italy. Even more renowned was his illustrious successor Rabbi Solomon bar Isaac, better known as Rashi.

51

Although born in Troyes, France, he pursued his religious studies in Worms, an indication of the great prestige that German centers of Jewish learning enjoyed in medieval times. Rashi's famous commentaries on the Old Testament and the Talmud influenced not only his coreligionists but Christian theologians as well, and are still cited today. Martin Luther, for example, referred to Rashi in translating the Old Testament into German, and scholars of all eras have used Rashi's critical commentaries and interpretations when they needed help in unraveling obscure biblical passages.

German rabbis maintained their leading role into the modern epoch. During the nineteenth century, the two most influential German rabbis were Abraham Geiger and Samson Raphael Hirsch. Although they were almost exact contemporaries and had even studied together, they became the leaders of two very different schools of Jewish thought. Geiger (born in Frankfurt, 1810, died in Berlin, 1874) was the founder of the Reform movement in Judaism. His writings had a profound influence on Jews not only in Germany but in Europe and America as well. Celebrated for his brilliant scholarship and critical capacity, he was the most outstanding exponent of the liberal tendencies in modern Jewish thought. His major work, *Urschrift und Übersetzung der Bibel* ("Original Text and Translation of the Bible"), published in 1857, excited the greatest interest.

Samson Raphael Hirsch (born in Hamburg, 1808, died in Frankfurt, 1888) started out as a friend of Geiger's, but he began to hold quite different views on

Judaism and became the leader of the neo-Orthodox movement and hostile to the liberal tendencies that Geiger upheld. But he also differed from strict Orthodox Jews, especially Zionists, who emphasized the distinct national character of Judaism. Seeing the Jews not as a nation but as a purely religious community, Hirsch believed there was no reason why pious Jews observing all the commandments should not adjust to the political and social institutions of the country in which they were living. His ideas are expounded in his books *Nineteen Letters* (1836) and *Horab* (1837).

During the twentieth century, the two most important German Jewish religious figures were Franz Rosenzweig and Leo Baeck. Rosenzweig (born in Kassel, 1886, died in Frankfurt, 1929), like many other German Jews, grew up in an atmosphere of assimilation; indeed, in 1913, having studied philosophy in Freiburg and Berlin, he was on the verge of converting to Christianity. But when he attended religious services on the eve of Yom Kippur, the high Holy Day of Atonement, he was so deeply moved by the experience that he abandoned all thought of conversion and began his studies of Hebrew and the Jewish tradition. His sense of being a Jew was further strengthened during World War I when, as a soldier on the Eastern Front, he came into contact with the Jewish communities in Poland. Out of these encounters came his major book, *The Star of Redemption* (1921), in which he argued that true religion was not only moral behavior or observance of Jewish law, but also a spiritual faith and a personal relationship to God which shapes all our life and thinking.

Leo Baeck (born in Lissa in the province of Posen, 1873, died in London, 1956), represents yet another aspect of modern Jewish thought. Deeply influenced by the neo-Kantian Hermann Cohen, he, like Mendelssohn, believed that Judaism was the religion of reason, an argument he expounded in his *The Essence of Judaism* (1905). A man of great learning and moral character, Baeck was the leader of the Jewish community in Berlin from 1912 until 1943, when he was sent to the Nazi concentration camp at Theresienstadt. Although he had long realized the danger threatening the Jews in Nazified Germany, he had not left the country, choosing instead to stay in Berlin in order to help his congregation. After the war, however, he settled in London, where he spent the rest of his life. The Leo Baeck Institute, devoted to the study of German Jews, was established after his death; it has branches in New York, London, and Jerusalem.

The best known of the modern Jewish religious thinkers is undoubtedly Martin Buber, whose writings on religion, philosophy, sociology, psychology, and mythology have influenced the religious and secular thought of both Jews and non-Jews throughout the world. Although he was not a native of Germany, Buber should be seen in a German Jewish context, for he spent most of his life in Germany and wrote in the German language.[1]

54

Martin (Mordecai) Buber was born in Vienna in 1878, but he grew up with his grandparents in Lemberg (Lvov) in eastern Galicia, at that time part of the Austro-Hungarian empire. His paternal grandfather, Salomon Buber, was a noted Biblical scholar and a prominent member of the Jewish community, and it was through him that the young Buber was introduced to Hebrew and Biblical scholarship. But even more important to his intellectual growth was the influence of his grandmother, who taught him to love literature, especially the German classics. He was tutored at home until he was ten, and then attended the gymnasium in Lemberg. His everyday life made him multilingual: the Buber family spoke German; the Jewish community in Lemberg spoke Yiddish; instruction at the gymnasium was in Polish; and the language of the synagogue was Hebrew. In addition to these languages, the young Buber also mastered Greek, which became his favorite language, and Latin, French, Italian, and Dutch.

In 1896, when he was eighteen years old, Buber left Lemberg for Vienna, where he enrolled at the university. At that time, Vienna was a great cultural center, and the young Buber entered the intellectual life of the Austrian capital with great enthusiasm. Such eminent writers as Hugo von Hofmannsthal, Richard Beer-Hofmann, and Arthur Schnitzler befriended him, and he discovered the work of Stefan George and Friedrich Nietzsche. Stimulated by the Viennese environment, he began writing poems and essays. In 1897, he left Vienna for Leipzig to study under Wilhelm Wundt, who was the most famous psychologist of the day. In Leipzig, Buber joined the liberal Ethical Culture Society, where he gave a number of well-received lectures on Ferdinand Lassalle which established him as one of the most brilliant young men in Leipzig's Jewish community.

It was during these years that Buber also became interested in Zionism. Although he was not at this time deeply religious, or even especially observant of Judaism, he nevertheless felt an affinity with the Jewish people and with Jewish tradition. In 1898, he became the head of the student Zionist organization in Leipzig and invited Theodor Herzl to address its members. His enthusiasm for the Zionist ideals is expressed in a Purim prologue which he wrote for the Jewish Union of Berlin:

> Today slaves, tomorrow we shall be masters!
> This year in narrow, sunless strangeness,
> Next year in our fatherland![2]

In 1901, Herzl asked Buber to become the editor of his official Zionist journal, but this association was brief. Buber and Herzl disagreed over the question of whether the goal of Zionism should be the cultural rebirth of the Jewish people or the establishment of a Jewish state with the help of the great world powers, and Buber soon became estranged from Herzl's political Zionism.

After that, he turned increasingly to the study of mysticism, which would become his main field. His doctoral dissertation was on the fifteenth-century Catholic mystic Nicholas de Cusa and the seventeenth-century Lutheran mystic Jacob Boehme. In 1909, he brought together descriptions of mystical experiences from different periods and cultures in a volume entitled *Ecstatic Confessions*, which was followed the next year by a book on the Chinese mystic Lao-tzu and the teachings of the Tao. He also became interested in Hindu mysticism and increasingly in the great thirteenth-century German mystic Meister Eckhard. However, it was the Hasidic mystics of eighteenth-century Poland whom he found most inspiring, and it was principally their life and writings that Buber devoted himself to during much of this period.

Using the traditional sayings of the Hasidic *Zaddikim* ("holy men"), whose works he rewrote in modern German, Buber published *The Tales of Rabbi Nachman* in 1907 and *The Legend of Baal-Schlem* in 1908. Although some Jewish scholars criticized his interpretation of the Hasidic material, these works aroused great interest among young Jewish intellectuals who were looking for a better understanding of their Jewish heritage, as well as among non-Jews interested in mysticism. He also gave many lectures on Hasidism and Jewish thought, which were transcribed and published in two volumes. In Berlin, where he had moved during this time, he became an outstanding member of the Jewish community and was revered by many young Jewish intellectuals.

The years of World War I were decisive ones for Buber's intellectual development. Unlike his close friend the pacifist Gustav Landauer, who had opposed the war from the start, Buber initially supported the German cause. In fact, he was disappointed when he was declared unfit to serve in the army. Like most German Jews, he identified himself with the German nation. He also hoped that, as a result of the war, Central Europe and especially the Jews of Poland and Russia would be liberated and that Palestine would be freed for Jewish regeneration. However, as the war dragged on without any of his hopes nearing realization, he became increasingly hostile to the German war effort. An outward sign of this change was in 1916 when he moved to Heppenheim an der Bergstrasse because he found the warlike atmosphere of the capital unbearable.

That same year, Buber joined the Jewish National Committee and became editor of its influential monthly magazine, *Der Jude*. Under his direction, the journal enjoyed great success and was considered the leading publication of the German-speaking Jews. It advocated equal rights for the Jews and regarded them as a nation like other nations with its own spiritual and cultural identity. Like the Zionists, it was opposed to both the ideals of the Enlightenment and the complete assimilation of the Jews. Many of its pages were devoted to Jewish settlements in Palestine and Jews of Poland, Galicia, and Lithuania, as well as to Hasidic stories. The magazine was the first to take up the problem of Arabs in Palestine, a subject which was to be one of Buber's chief concerns in later years.

In 1923, at the age of forty-five, Buber published

what was to be his single most influential work, *Ich und Du* ("I and Thou"), on which he had been working for many years. In it, he discusses all the problems that had long concerned him and sets forth new spiritual and philosophical insights. The book's central theme is that through dialogue between the "I" and the "Thou," man could reach out to both God and other human beings. In contrast to his earlier thinking, which had been concerned with the mystical union of the human soul with the godhead, he now taught that the relationship between the "I" and the deity also involves the relationship among humans, as well as between mankind and the world.

A profound and original work, *Ich und Du* established Buber's reputation internationally, among Jews and non-Jews. It deals with all the problems of human existence; with creation, revelation, and redemption; with the Eternal Thou and the Jewish Jesus and the Pauline Christ; with knowledge and its limitations; with psychology and psychotherapy; with politics and community, love and marriage, art and music. To Buber, God is the "Wholly Other" and at the same time the "Wholly Same" who is present in all creation. Although *Ich und Du* is based on the Jewish tradition and the Bible, it nevertheless transcends both; as his most perceptive biographer, Maurice Friedman, writes: "*I and Thou* is unthinkable without the wisdom of Hasidism and the Hebrew Bible; it is in its form and its intent a universal book. It does not address itself to Jews as Jews, and even when it thinks in terms of community and history, it has no concern other than that of modern western man.">³

The decade between the publication of *I and Thou* and Hitler's rise to power in 1933 was the high point in Martin Buber's life. No German Jew since Moses Mendelssohn, some hundred fifty years earlier, had enjoyed such universal renown and admiration. As a writer and teacher, he had a major role in the Germany of the Weimar Republic, and, when he celebrated his fiftieth birthday in 1928, the event was commemorated by festivities and with several publications honoring this great religious thinker and illustrious man.

During these years, Buber was less active in the Zionist cause, as his ideas for the future of Palestine were not accepted by the World Zionist Congress. In contrast to the dominant majority, he advocated a binational state in which Jews and Arabs would live in harmony, with neither trying to dominate the other, a policy that was supported by the Brit Shalom, or Convenant of Peace group, of which Buber was then a member. Behind the scenes, he also fought against the Zionist Revisionists, who demanded a Jewish Legion and wanted a Jewish-only Palestine, which would include the present-day Jordan. Although the Revisionists, under the leadership of Vladimir Jabotinsky, seceded from the Zionist World Congress, its ideas were carried on by the Herut Freedom Party, of which Menachem Begin became the leader.

Buber was also very active in this decade as a teacher in Frankfurt at the Jüdische Lehrhaus, which had been founded by his close friend Franz Rosenzweig, and later at Frankfurt University, where he was first lecturer of Jewish philosophy and ethics and later professor of history and religion. In addition to his teaching posts, he worked with the Odenwald Schule, a school well-known for it experimental educational program, and gave numerous lectures and participated in many conferences there. At the same time, he conducted an extensive correspondence with the numerous people who turned to him for guidance and advice.

A man of extraordinary energy, Buber found time in the midst of all these activities to undertake a new translation of the Old Testament into German at the request of a German publisher. While Mendelssohn had translated it into a German transcribed in Hebrew characters in order to acquaint the Jews with the German language, Buber's purpose was exactly the opposite: to make it as close to Hebrew as possible in order to bring assimilated Jews closer to the original text. Rosenzweig assisted him in this project, but it was such a vast undertaking that it was not completed until 1961, long after Rosenzweig's death. But sections of the work were being published as soon as Buber and Rosenzweig finished them, so this fresh translation was already making its mark on both Jewish and Christian scholarly circles in Germany at that time.

Buber made his first trip to Palestine in 1927, a visit he undertook with his wife (although she was born a Catholic, she had converted to Judaism). He was impressed with the *kibbutzim* and took an active interest in the development of Hebrew University in Jerusalem.

At this point, he had not yet thought of settling in Palestine, but when the possibility of the chairmanship of the religious faculty arose, he responded enthusiastically, only to have the offer withdrawn after opposition from Orthodox rabbis. The suggestion of his friend Juda Leib Magnes, the chancellor of Hebrew University, to make him life rector also came to nothing, again despite Buber's own interest in the idea.

While he was, of course, primarily a Jewish thinker, Buber was also in close contact with Christian theologians. He corresponded and exchanged ideas with men such as Albert Schweizer, whom he admired above all the others, Paul Tillich, Emil Brunner, and the Catholic theologian Witig. In fact, his views were more acceptable in some ways to many Christians than they were to Orthodox Jews, who resented his rejection of traditional laws. Also highly offensive to the Jewish community was his interpretation of the position of Jesus:

> He is the first in the series of men who, stepping out of the hiddeness of the servant of the Lord, the real Messianic mystery, acknowledge their Messiaship in their souls and words. This first one in the series was incomparably the purest, the most legitimate, the most endowed with real Messianic power.[4]

The events of 1933 came to Buber, as to many German Jews, like a bolt out of the blue. He was aware of anti-Semitism in Germany, but the temperaments and beliefs of his German colleagues and friends were so removed from it, that nothing they did could prepare him for the terrible events which were to occur. At first he could not believe what was happening, but after the so-called Nuremberg Laws were passed in 1935, stripping German Jews of all their rights as citizens, he realized the true dimension of the nightmare that was enveloping the German Jewish community. Although many of his Christian friends stood by him, he felt more and more isolated. He was dismissed from his professorship at Frankfurt University and eventually he was not even permitted to give public lectures. His last years in Germany, between 1933 and 1938, were taken up with work on behalf of Jewish cultural organizations and with his attempts to instill pride and dignity in his fellow Jews in the face of the catastrophe. Finally, only weeks before Kristallnacht put an end to the German Jewish community, Buber left Germany for the land of his ancestors.

He arrived in Palestine in 1938, shortly after his sixtieth birthday, and settled in the suburbs of Jerusalem. Unlike many other refugees who had lost everything, Buber had been able to bring out his huge library and his furniture, and he at once received an appointment as a professor of the sociology of religion at Hebrew University. He was also fortunate in having both of his children, as well as his grandchildren, join him in Palestine. His first task was to learn modern Hebrew, but since he was well versed in ancient Hebrew, he soon mastered the modern form and was able to write and lecture in the new language. In fact, his first years in Palestine were quite happy, although he was troubled by the deteriorating relationship between Jews and Arabs.

Buber resumed his career both as a teacher and an author with renewed vigor, and in 1942 his book *Prophetic Faith* was published in Hebrew. This was followed by the novel *Gog and Magog* in 1943, which he regarded as one of his most important works. It first appeared as a serial in a Hebrew newspaper and later came out in book form in both Hebrew and in German. A historical novel based on Hasidic tales, it expressed many of the ideas he held most dear, but it never had the impact of such major works as *I and Thou*.

While his life in his new homeland was peaceful and rewarding, Buber was horrified by the war with its terrible slaughter and the destruction of the European Jewish communities. When the first reports of the Holocaust reached him, he simply could not accept them, for he did not believe that Germans could be capable of such horrifying atrocities. He was not persuaded of the accuracy of these accounts until 1945, when the truth about the extermination camps and gas oven was forced into the open and confirmed.

For one so deeply committed to Jewish-Arab cooperation, these years were also made difficult as terrorists from both sides fought each other. The chance of cooperation grew ever smaller and was extinguished when a nationalistic Israeli state was established instead of the binational one Buber had envisaged.

After the war, Buber renewed his relationships with his colleagues in Europe. In 1947, when he was almost seventy, he went on a lecture tour, giving no fewer than sixty lectures at different universities in Holland, Belgium, Sweden, Denmark, France, and England, all of which were greeted with enthusiasm. He was not, however, willing to go to Germany at this time, although he did contact his German publisher and received hundreds of letters from German friends and admirers on the occasion of his seventieth birthday. The German Christian theologians, especially, feeling a deep sense of guilt over the atrocities of the Hitler years, tried to establish a dialogue with the great Jewish thinker. There was, in fact, a renewed interest in Buber and his works across Germany. When Hamburg University awarded him the prestigious Goethe prize in 1951, Buber finally visited Germany for the first time since his departure. Even more significant, in 1953, he received the Peace Prize of the German Book Trade, an occasion celebrated by a solemn ceremony at St. Paul's Church in Frankfurt, which was attended by thousands of Germans, including Theodor Heuss, then the president of the German Federal Republic (West Germany). Characteristically, Buber donated the prize money which he received for better Jewish-Arab understanding. However, the fact that he not only visited Germany but accepted such a prize, and accepted it in a Christian church, aroused angry protest not only in Israel but also in the Jewish press of Switzerland and the United States.

As busy as he was in the late 1940s and the 1950s with teaching and lecturing, he continued to write prolifically, producing several books of Hasidic tales and works on Hasidism that were published in Hebrew, German, and English and enjoyed great popularity. Equally important were his works dealing with Judaism and the Jewish-Christian dialogue. His wide interests are evident in his 1947 book on Moses in which he rejected Freud's psychoanalytic interpretation of the great Jewish prophet,[5] and in his *Two Types of Faith*, in which he discussed the relationship between Jesus and Paul, demonstrating that Jesus reflected the Jewish tradition, while Paul introduced into early Christianity alien elements derived from Classical sources. In his *Paths in Utopia*, he attacked the centralized Socialism of Marx and Lenin and advocated instead a democratic, cooperative socialism.

Buber had been virtually unknown in the United States before the 1950s, but now he made three lecture tours to America. In 1951, he spoke at the Jewish Theological Seminary in New York; in 1957, he gave talks on philosophical anthropology at the Washington School of Psychiatry at the invitation of Harry Starck Sullivan; and in 1958, Princeton University appointed him research scholar. He also gave lectures from New England to California, and many of his books appeared in American editions and attained widespread popularity.

When Buber celebrated his eightieth birthday in 1958, congratulations and good wishes poured in from all over the world. The occasion was celebrated with special observances in Israel and the United States, and

Festschriften were published in Germany. In Paris, the Sorbonne conferred an honorary doctorate on him, and Heidelberg University also gave him an honorary degree. Cologne University established a Martin Buber chair of Jewish Studies, Munich gave him the Culture Prize of the city, and he received the Schweitzer medal. Five years later, in 1963, the Dutch awarded him the Erasmus Prize for his contribution to the spiritual life of Europe, and the American Academy of Arts and Sciences elected him as its first Israeli member. He was also twice nominated for a Nobel Prize; for literature by his colleagues at Hebrew University, and for peace by Dag Hammarskjold.

In Israel, however, Buber remained a controversial figure for several reasons. Not only had he advocated a binational state and favored closer cooperation between Jews and Arabs, but he had also been harshly critical of Jewish extremists. Another issue was the controversial position he had taken on the trial of Nazi war criminal Adolf Eichmann, whom Israeli agents had brought to Israel in 1960 to stand trial; first Buber advocated trying him before an international tribunal, and then he urged that his death sentence be commuted to life imprisonment. His position on the Cold War was no less controversial: he recommended dialogue instead of confrontation and favored total nuclear disarmament. Finally, Orthodox Jews felt that he misread the Bible; and some scholars were of the opinion that, while his Hasidic tales might make good literature, they were not in the spirit of the true Hasidic tradition.

When Buber died at the age of eighty-seven, on June 13, 1965, he was without doubt the most famous Jew in the world and the most distinguished and revered, though controversial, citizen of Israel. The first person to offer condolences at his house in Talbiyeh was Zalman Shazar, the president of Israel, while David Ben-Gurion, his old political opponent, and Shmuel Agnon, the Israeli author and Nobel laureate, sat *shivah* for five hours by his dead body. All classes were canceled at Hebrew University; hundreds of students filed past his body and thousands of friends and admirers, both Jewish and gentile, paid tribute to this great and good man. The eulogy at his funeral was delivered by Levi Eshkol, the prime minister of Israel, and messages of condolence were received from people all over the world, including such well-known figures as Konrad Adenauer, Dean Rusk, and Adlai Stevenson.

Although Martin Buber died a generation ago, his spirit lives on. His books are still read, for they embody the best of the Jewish spiritual tradition with the best of German culture.

NOTES

[1] There is a vast literature on Buber and his thought in both German and English. See, e.g.: Hans Kohn, *Martin Buber, sein Werk und seine Zeit* (1930); W. Nig, *Martin Bubers Weg in Unserer Zeit* (1940); Maurice Friedman, *Martin Buber's Life and Work*, 3 vols. (New York: Dutton, 1981-83); M. Diamond, *Martin Buber, Jewish Existentialist* (1968); and W. Manheim, *Martin Buber* (1968). See also: *The Letters of Martin Buber:*

A Life of Dialogue (New York,1991); and Maurice Friedman, *Encounter on a Narrow Ridge: A Life of Martin Buber* (New York: Paragon House, 1991).

[2] Friedman, *The Early Years (1878-1923)*. Vol. 1 of *Martin Buber's Life and Work*, p. 43.

[3] Friedman, vol 1., 322-23.

[4] Buber, *The Origins and Meaning of Hasidism,* trans. Maurice Friedman (New York: Harper, 1960) 250.

[5] See Sigmund Freud, *Moses and Monotheism*. Vol. 23 of *The Complete Psychological Works of Sigmund Freud* (Standard Edition), trans. James Strachey (London and New York: The Hogarth Press, 1939).

KARL MARX

III: SOCIAL SCIENCES

Another area to which German Jews made outstanding contributions is the social sciences. In law, political science, economics, and sociology, many of the principal thinkers of the nineteenth and twentieth century were either Jews or men from Jewish backgrounds. This is not surprising in light of the fact that the traditional Jewish studies often dealt with legal and social questions in connection with biblical precepts and the teaching of the Talmud. Interestingly enough, these Jewish scholars were by no means all of one persuasion; they ranged from true conservatives who wished to preserve the existing social order to extreme radicals who called for drastic changes or revolution. Some were pragmatists who thought in concrete, down-to-earth terms, while others were utopian, envisioning an ideal society of complete justice, equality, and free-

71

dom. They were also equally diverse in their relationships to their Jewish heritage; there were those who emphasized their roots with pride, while others either ignored or concealed their Jewish origin.

A typical example of the second group, and one of the first German Jews to win renown in law, was Friedrich Julius Schlesinger (born in Munich, 1802, died in Brückenau, Bavaria, 1861). Like many Jews who wanted to assimilate completely, he changed his name—from Schlesinger to Stahl. In 1819, at the age of seventeen, he also converted to Christianity. Hence the door to academic advancement was opened to him, and he became a professor of Roman and ecclesiastical law, first in Munich, later in Erlangen and Würzburg, and finally in Berlin. He also became a member of the legislative chamber and was elected to the Prussian Synod of the Lutheran Church. His most significant contribution was his 1929 book *Philosophy of Law of the State based on Protestant Christian Principles*. An extreme conservative, Stahl joined the Conservative Party and in 1849 became a leader in the upper house of the Prussian parliament. He carried his Prussian identification so far that he became one of the authors of the so-called Tivoli program of the Conservative Party which, among other things, opposed the emancipation of the Jews; although unlike Hitler and the anti-Semites of later times, he and his contemporaries favored the conversion of Jews to Christianity on the grounds that such a step would remove any stigma attached to their Jewish birth.

72

The exact opposite, both in his political ideas and in his relationship to his Jewish origin, was Moritz Hess (born in Bonn, 1812, died in Paris, 1875). In contrast to Stahl, who dropped his Jewish name in order to appear more German, Hess changed his first name from Moritz to Moses so as to identify more closely with his roots. Although he came from an Orthodox family, the young Hess showed little interest in Judaism. When he was a student at Bonn University, he married a young Christian woman and threw himself heart and soul into the socialist movement. He became editor, with Karl Marx, of the radical newspaper *Rheinische Zeitung* and was active in the uprising of 1848. After the failed Frankfurt Parliament, Hess had to flee Prussia. He wandered around Europe for several years, and in 1853 settled in Paris, where he remained for the rest of his life. Hess differed from Marx in basing his socialism on humanitarian rather than economic grounds; he believed that socialism would come about through educating the people and organizing workers. His most lasting contribution, however, came not so much out of his activities as an early Socialist as it did out of his anticipation of the Zionist ideals of Theodor Herzl. In 1862, he wrote *Rome and Jerusalem*, in which he advocated the establishment of a Jewish homeland in Palestine. For him, Jews represented a separate nation; far from advocating assimilation into German culture, he believed that the Jewish people, like other peoples, should develop and maintain their own distinctive characteristics.

Different from either Stahl or Hess was Eduard

Bernstein (born in Berlin, 1850, died in Berlin, 1932). He started out as an employee of a bank but, in 1871, when he was only twenty-one, he joined the Social Democratic Party, to which he devoted most of his time and energy for the rest of his life. In keeping with the principles of the party, he severed his relationship with the Jewish community although he returned to it in his old age. Due to anti-socialist laws of 1878, he had to leave Germany, and went into exile, first to Switzerland, where he edited a socialist newspaper, and then to London. However, in 1901, he was permitted to return to Germany, where for many years he served as a member of the Reichstag, the German parliament. He was a leader of the Social Democratic Party in Germany from 1902 to 1928, with the exception of some of the war years when the party ousted him because of his pacifist stand.

Bernstein's principal contribution was to socialist theory. But he differed from Marx, who believed that a society based in capitalism would eventually have only two classes—a vast proletariat of wage slaves and a few wealthy and powerful capitalists—at which point the proletariat would become revolutionary and seize power. Bernstein, on the other hand, believed that the middle class, far from vanishing into the ranks of the proletariat, would continue to flourish. He maintained that socialism would be brought about by gradual change, rather than by a class struggle and a violent overthrow of the existing order. As the editor of the *Sozialistische Monatshefte*, Bernstein played a prominent role in German socialist circles. He fostered the position that the Social Democrats should join forces with other political parties whose goals were similar. Bernstein and his followers became known as revisionists, to distinguish them from orthodox Marxists. Even among the Social Democratic Party of Germany, his ideas provoked a bitter controversy, for although they were rejected by the party's leaders, they had a marked influence on party members, not only in Germany but in other European countries as well. Of Bernstein's books, the two most influential are *Evolutionary Socialism* (1898), in which he set forth his criticism of Marxism, and *My Years in Exile* (1921).

Because many of the leading social scientists in Germany of the twentieth century were Jews, great numbers of political scientists, economists, and sociologists who had been prominent in the Weimar Republic were forced to leave the country after Hitler's rise to power. But they went on to make significant contributions in their new homes, be it Palestine, the United States, or another European country. The most influential of these German Jewish emigrés in the social sciences was probably the sociologist and historian Karl Mannheim. Born in Budapest in 1893, he was educated in Germany, where he had a distinguished career before being discharged by Nazi authorities. As a young man, he studied in Berlin and Paris, and then at the Heidelberg University under Max Weber, the most famous German sociologist of his day. In 1926, he was appointed lecturer at the university in Heidelberg. In 1930, he moved to Frankfurt University, where he became one of the luminaries of the so-called Frankfurt School of social scientists. In 1933, at the age of forty, Mannheim left Germany for England, where he was appointed to a professorship at the London School of Economics and Political Science. He taught there until his death at age fifty-four, in 1947.

In his work, Mannheim emphasized the interconnection between historical and social facts on the one hand and thoughts and ideas on the other, developing the school of thought known as philosophical sociology. He was a prolific writer in both German and English, as well as the editor of the journals *International Library of Sociology* and *Social Reconstruction*. Among his most important books are *Ideology and Utopia* (1929) and *Introduction to the Sociology of Knowledge* (1936).

It is said that a thinker has achieved the height of recognition in his or her field when that person enters history as an eponym. It is no exaggeration to say that Karl Marx is more famous and has exerted a more lasting influence—not only on German culture, but on the entire world—than any other German Jew. Worshipped like a god at one extreme and damned as a demon at the other, Marx has had a dramatic impact on our entire era. He has been revered by countless people both in the West and the East; in China, a giant portrait of Marx, along with one of his close friend Friedrich Engels, still stands in the great square outside of the main gate of the Imperial Palace in Peking. In the early twentieth century, Marxism became the philosophical foundation of one of the most powerful governments in the world.

Biographies and memoirs of Marx exist in the hundreds. His own writings, published only in small editions during his lifetime, have been reprinted in millions of copies and translated into all major languages. Complete editions of his works have been issued in Germany and in Russia, and his letters, especially those to Engels, have been published in a variety of editions.[1]

Karl Marx was born on May fifth, 1818, in Trier, an ancient and beautiful city in the Mosel valley. His father—a successful and much esteemed lawyer and a typical man of the Enlightenment who admired French culture and philosophy—had converted to Christianity in 1817 and changed his first name from Herschel to the German Heinrich. Karl's paternal grandfather had been a rabbi; in fact, Marx came from a long line of rabbis on both sides of his family, among them, Meir Katzenellenbogen, head of the Talmudic school in Padua in the sixteenth century. Karl himself was baptized into Christianity at the age of six, when he was about to enter school. Although he was aware of his distinguished ancestors, his Jewish heritage—and for that matter, his family's adopted Christianity—meant very little to him. Marx's attitude toward all religions was highly critical, for he regarded all religions as "opiates of the people." As he said in an essay on G.W.F. Hegel, "The abolition of religion, as the illusory happiness of the people, is the demand for their real happiness. The demand to abandon the illusions about their condition is a demand to abandon a condition which requires illusions."[2] Marx's rejection of all religion notwithstanding, his temperament and his pronouncements in many ways remind one of the Old Testament prophets: his thundering against the wickedness and corruption of the bourgeoisie, his castigations of the people for their worship of the Golden Calf, and his vision of the proletariat as the new Chosen People who will lead us out of the desert to a perfect society where justice and happiness will reign.

Marx's only writing on Jews and Judaism was an essay consisting of a review of two works by the German philosopher Bruno Bauer, which was first published in the journal *Deutsch-Französische Jahrbücher* in 1844, when he was twenty-five years old. In it, he says:

> Let us consider the real worldly Jews, not the Sabbath Jews, as Bauer does, but the everyday Jews. We will not look for the secret of the Jew in his religion, but we will look for the secret of religion in the real Jew. What is the secular basis of Judaism? Practical needs, egoism. What is the secular cult of the Jew? Huckstering. What is his secular God? Money. Very well. Emancipation from huckstering and money, and therefor from practical, real Judaism would be the self-emancipation of our epoch. An organization of society, which would abolish the fundamental conditions of huckstering, would render the Jew impossible. His religious consciousness would dissolve like a mist in the real vital air of society.[3]

This total rejection of the Jewish faith and the Jewish people was also reflected in Marx's relationship to eminent fellow Jews in the socialist movement. For example, after initially befriending Hess, Marx later broke with him because of Hess's emphasis of his Jewish roots. He saw the Hegelian socialist Ferdinand Lassalle as a rival, and in a letter to Engels described him as "a typical Jew from the Slavic border, always ready to exploit everyone for his private ends."[4]

The young Marx attended the gymnasium in Trier, where he was an outstanding pupil; he studied law at the university in Bonn. Since the year he spent there was apparently devoted to drink and pleasures, his father decided to send him to the Jena University in Berlin, which was considered a much more serious and demanding academy. But even here Marx attended lectures only rarely and did little academic work, spending most of his time reading extracurricular works and frequenting coffee houses, which had become very popular with the intelligentsia. He spent five years in Berlin, during which time he changed his course of study from law to philosophy. In 1841, with a thesis titled *Differences between the Natural Philosophy of Democritus and the Natural Philosophy of Epicurus*, he received his Ph.D. from Jena.

The greatest influence on Marx during these Berlin years was the philosophy of Hegel. Although Georg Wilhelm Friedrich Hegel had been dead for a decade, his ideas still dominated the thinking at Jena University. It was there that Marx first became associated with a group known as the Young Hegelians. Marx was greatly influenced by Hegel's notions of dialectics and his philosophy of state. Yet writing in 1873, he said:

> My dialectic method is not only different from the Hegelian, but is its direct opposite. To Hegel, the life-process of the human brain, *i.e.*, the process of thinking, which, under the name of 'the idea,' he even transforms into an independent subject, is the demiurgos of the real world, and the real world is only the external, phenomenal form of 'the Idea.' With me, on the contrary, the ideal is nothing else than the material world reflected by the human mind, and translated into forms of thought.[5]

Marx had hoped to pursue an academic career. At the time he took his degree, it seemed as if there was a possibility of his being appointed a lecturer in Bonn through the intercession of his friend Bruno Bauer, but when Bauer got into trouble because of his atheism, the opportunity for Marx disappeared, and he turned to journalism. In 1842, he became editor of the journal *Rheinische Zeitung*, when he was only twenty-six years old. But the radical tone of the publication soon stirred up criticism, and it was suppressed by the government the following year. Marx then went to Paris. One of the two most important events at this stage of Marx's life took place in 1843 in Paris—he met Friedrich Engels, who was to become his closest friend, his collaborator, and his main financial support.

The second major event was his marriage that same year to Jenny von Westphalen, a daughter of the Prussian aristocracy whose brother became the Prussian minister of the interior and whose grandmother had been an Argyll, one of the most ancient and noble of the Scottish clans. Her father had been a neighbor of the Marx family in Trier, and the young Marx had greatly admired him. Jenny herself was a beautiful and intelligent young woman, four years Marx's senior, whom Marx had been in love with ever since he was seventeen. The marriage was disapproved of by both families because of the difference in their social positions and ages, but it turned out to be a very happy one. His beloved Jenny willingly shared all the difficulties and deprivations of his life, and together they had six children.

Marx hoped to continue his literary activities in the French capital, with plans to edit a journal with his friend Arnold Ruge which they called *German-French Annals*. They managed to publish only one volume, which contained Marx's *Outline of a Critique of Hegel's Philosophy* and *On the Jewish Question*; Engels' *Outline of a Critique of Political Economy and the Position of England*; and Thomas Carlyle's *Past and Present*. Marx also contributed to the socialist paper *Vorwärts*, most notably a report on the revolt of the weavers in Silesia. Soon, however, under pressure from the Prussian government, the French authorities expelled Marx, and he and Jenny moved to Brussels in February, 1845.

Marx's stay in Belgium, where Friedrich Engels joined him, was also in jeopardy, so he renounced his Prussian citizenship in order to avoid being deported again, a step he was to regret later in life. Nevertheless, this period was a very productive time, for he wrote *Holy Family* and *Theses on Feuerbach*; and, with Engels, *Ger-*

man Ideology, in which he explained his idea of dialectical materialism. Even more important for the direction of his future career, he and Engels visited England, where they met leaders of the workers' political reform organization known as Chartists, as well as the members of the League of the Just. In 1847, he and Engels wrote the *Communist Manifesto* which was produced at the request of the Communist League of London and published in the German language in London in 1848, when Marx was thirty years old. With it, Marx established himself as one of the principal ideologues and spokesmen of the communist movement.

Marx's earlier writings had been issued in small editions which found few readers, either in his day or our own, but the *Communist Manifesto* was read widely at the time and has been ever since. It has been translated into every major language. Beginning with, "A spectre haunts Europe—the spectre of communism" and ending with the words, "Let the ruling classes tremble at the prospect of a communist revolution. Proletarians have nothing to lose but their chains," the Manifesto is a bold and exciting attack on the bourgeoisie and the evils of capitalism as well as a call to revolution. As Marx writes in another place: "Philosophers have sought to interpret the world in various ways. The point, however, is to change it!"

The Manifesto calls upon the proletariat in all countries to organize as an international class. It also advocates the destruction of the bourgeoisie, with the working class seizing power. Private property should be abolished and the means of production taken over by the workers for the benefit of all. The goals of communists should be the same everywhere, Marx maintained, for workers belong to no country and will wipe out all the distinctions among the bourgeois nations. According to Marx, all human history is the history of class struggle. He argued that the bourgeoisie, which by then had replaced the feudal aristocracy as the ruling class, was reaching its end as high man on the totem pole and would inevitably be replaced by the proletariat. The antagonism between the bourgeoisie and the working class, he said, was steadily increasing because society was being split into two great hostile camps with wealth and the means of production concentrated in the hands of fewer and fewer capitalists, while the mass of the people were becoming dispossessed, powerless proletarians. According to Marx's dialectical materialism, change comes about as a result of "the struggle of opposites." The existing order (the bourgeois state) will be brought down by the proletarian revolution—its "antithesis," or opposite, which will be followed by a new, revolutionary order, or "synthesis."

The year 1848 was important not only for the publication of the *Communist Manifesto*, but also for political events in Europe which affected Marx's personal life. He was expelled from Belgium and returned to Paris, where a revolution had broken out and where he was elected chairman of the Communist League. In April of 1848, he returned to his native Rhineland. There, he and Engels took part in the revolutionary uprisings and edited a radical newspaper called *Neue Rheinische Zeitung.* But following the defeat of the revolution the next year, Marx was tried for inciting to revolt and his newspaper was suppressed. Although he was acquitted at his trial, he left his native country for good in August 1849. At the age of thirty-one, he and Jenny and their children settled in London, where he spent the rest of his life. Still, he never became a British citizen or identified with the English people; he continued to regard himself as a German exile, and associated largely with other Germans, and wrote in his native language.

The years in England were very difficult for Marx and his family. For some years they lived in a cramped apartment in Soho and were often reduced to near starvation. Their livelihood depended largely on the help and support of relatives and friends, notably the ever generous Friedrich Engels. Marx's principal source of income was the meager pay he received for writing dispatches on European politics for the New York *Tribune* and articles he turned out for various newspapers and magazines. He also published a book called *The Eighteenth Brumaire of Louis Bonaparte,* a vicious attack on the politics and career of Napoleon's nephew who was to become Emperor Napoleon III. At the same time, both he and Engels continued to be active in the Communist League, for which they wrote the *Address of the Central Committee to the Communist League.* However, the League was dissolved, at Marx's suggestion, in 1852. A decade later, in 1864, Marx helped to found its successor, the International Workers' Organization, or the First International, which held its organizational meeting in London the following year. He wrote the organization's inaugural address and drew up the provisional rules which insured that he would be in control and that the new International would follow his ideas and direction.

During the 1850s and 1860s between his thirtieth and fiftieth years, Marx refined his political and economic theories. Although he was besieged by creditors, attacked by his enemies, and stricken by the early deaths of three of his six children—most especially his beloved son Edgar who died at the age of eight—and suffering himself from chronic illness, he continued his work. Every morning, with the exception of Sundays which he and his family spent at Hempstead Heath, Marx took himself to the library at the British Museum, where he did his voluminous research until seven in the evening. A meticulous scholar who always felt that more material had to be consulted, and a perfectionist who kept revising and rewriting, his progress was slow; but his energy and drive were enormous, and he was determined to produce a work that would be for political economy what Darwin's *Origin of the Species* had been for biology.

The result of his labor was a view of the political and economic world and the forces shaping it which today we call Marxism. Nikolai Lenin gave one of the best definitions of Marxism:

> Marx was the genius who continued and completed the three chief ideological currents of the nineteenth century, represented respectively by the three most advanced countries of humanity: classical German philosophy, classical English political economy, and French Socialism combined with French revolutionary doctrines. The remarkable consistency and unity of conception of Marx's views, acknowledged even by his opponents,…their totality constitute modern materialism and modern scientific Socialism as the theory and programme of the labour movement in all the civilized countries of the world.[6]

In other words, Marx combined the dialectics of Hegel with the economic teachings of Adam Smith and David Ricardo and the revolutionary ideas of Pierre Joseph Proudhon.

Marx's major work, which came out of those years spent at the library of the British Museum, was his three-volume *Das Kapital*. The first volume was published in Hamburg in 1867 when he was forty-nine. The second and third volumes were still unfinished at the time of his death almost two decades later but completed by Engels on the basis of Marx's extensive notes and were published in 1885 and 1894. Although the work did not win the acclaim that Marx had expected—and initially, was not even very widely read— it gradually gained a respectful audience. The first volume especially had a decisive influence on Socialist thinking; it was translated into Russian in 1872, into French in 1873, and in 1887, after Marx's death, into English. When the first German edition of that first volume sold out, Marx prepared several revised editions to which he added new forewords.

A long, very scholarly work, *Das Kapital* has none of the compactness and elan of the *Communist Manifesto*; it analyzes and criticizes the capitalist system in laborious and minute detail. John Lewis, a leading Marxist scholar, summarizes the content of the work quite well:

> At the heart of *Capital* is the representation of man being dehumanized and destroyed by a tyrannical force of ac-quisitiveness that has arisen and grown all powerful within him. It controls his movements, usurps his life energies, and, as a capitalist, obsesses him with a compulsive drive towards accumulation. Few works of literature or studies of the sick mind have portrayed with comparable insight the destructive and dehumanizing character of the capitalist system. This is seen in its effect on the worker with terrifying clarity in the increasing mechanisation of the labor process.[7]

Already in Marx's day, economists found much to criticize in this work, especially the theory that all wealth is derived from labor, and that the difference between the value of what a worker produces and what he or she is paid ("surplus value") constitutes the profit of an unscrupulous entrepreneur. Sociologists have also objected that Marx erred when he predicted that the middle class would disappear, leaving a few rich capitalists and a great mass of proletarians. In fact, they conclude, just the opposite happened—as the workers in the advanced industrial countries became more prosperous, they moved up to the middle class. It has further been pointed out that the revolutions that Marx

87

believed would break out in industrialized, developed nations have actually taken place in the least developed countries. However true these criticisms may yet prove to be, *Das Kapital*, with its detailed statistics derived from official British reports of the time and its hair-raising accounts of child labor in nineteenth-century England, makes a powerful impression.

While the earlier socialists had based their utopian dreams on moral reform, Marx—who abhorred all sentimentality—put his socialist theories on a scientific basis. For him, the development of capitalism inevitably led to socialism; for just as the feudal rule was followed by the rise of the bourgeoisie, so inevitably the capitalist class would be succeeded by the proletariat who, he believed, would establish a better and more just social system.

While working on his magnum opus, Marx continued to be active in socialist politics. The First International met in Geneva in 1866, in Lausanne in 1867, and in Brussels the following year. Interesting enough, Marx agreed to represent the Russian section of the International at the Geneva conference, so he began studying the Russian language and the Russian economy. Although his exile prevented him from being active in Germany, he continued to exert a strong influence on the German labor movement.

The most dramatic events of this period for Marx took place in Paris, when the population erupted in rebellion after France's humiliating surrender that had ended the Franco-Prussian War. The popular insurrection came together under the socialist-led Paris Commune of 1871, which gained temporary control of the French capital. Marx wrote of the uprising and the Commune in his *Civil War in France*.

Marx's position as the undisputed ideologue and leader of the revolutionary proletariat did not go unchallenged. The Russian revolutionary Mikhail Bakunin, a remarkable and colorful figure who was active in the First International, attracted a great following with his doctrine of militant anarchism. A fellow German, Ferdinand Lassalle, who founded the first labor party in Germany and was enormously popular among the German workers, also split from Marx's ideology over the issue of nationalism. Marx's treatment of these two revolutionaries—who had both once supported him and shared many of his ideals—was one of the least attractive episodes in Marx's life. Jealous of their popularity and unwilling to tolerate any divergence from his own ideas, Marx saw them as competitors and villains and did everything in his power to destroy their reputations and influence. He succeeded in having Bakunin expelled from the International in 1872, and might have ruined Lassalle if the latter had not been killed in a duel in 1864.

In a way, Marx's attitude toward these two men, as well as toward many others whom he first befriended and then turned bitterly against, foreshadowed the Communist Party purges of the following century under Stalin in the Soviet Union. Even those who admire Marx and follow his teachings have always been disturbed by the fact that a man who dedicated his life to the betterment of humanity and was a devoted husband and father could exhibit such vindictiveness and rancor when dealing with fellow socialists who disagreed with him—not to mention his vituperations against all capitalists, whether liberal or conservative. John Lewis, who on the whole was a great admirer of Marx, has this to say about an attack Marx launched on another socialist, Wilhelm Weitling, "This outburst was characteristic of Marx. He appeared domineering, arrogant and dogmatic, but such boldness and ruthlessness were required to demolish the delusions of the age."[8]

Far more critical was the American Carl Shultz, the secretary of the International who was later to become United States senator and army general. As a young man, Shultz had met Marx; years later, in describing the event, he said, "Never have I met a man of such offensive, insupportable arrogance. No opinion which differed essentially from his own was accorded the honor of even a half-way respectful consideration. Everyone who disagreed with him was treated with scarcely veiled contempt. He answered all arguments which displeased him with biting scorn for the pitiable ignorance of those who advanced them, or with a libelous questioning of their motives. I still remember the cutting, scornful tone with which he uttered—I might almost say spat—the word bourgeois; and he denounced as bourgeois—that is to say as an unmistakable example of the lowest moral and spiritual stagnation—everyone who dared to oppose his opinions."[9]

Where politics were concerned, the last ten years of Marx's life were his most serene. He had withdrawn from active politics and was looked upon as an elder statesman of Socialism who was revered for his theoretical contributions, although he was not consulted much in the day-to-day politics of the socialist movement. In Germany, the Social Democrats and the followers of Lassalle had formed a united party under August Bebel and Karl Liebknecht and pursued a Reformist program, not much to Marx's liking. The most interesting work he did in this period was the 1882 foreword that he wrote with Engels for the Russian edition of the *Communist Manifesto*. In it, they described Russian socialists and workers as leading the revolutionary movement in Europe.

But these were not easy years either. Plagued by new illnesses, Marx frequently had to visit baths on the continent. In 1881, his beloved Jenny died, and two years later he buried their eldest daughter. On March 4, 1883 Karl Marx himself died. He was buried at the Highgate Cemetery in London. Engels gave the gravesite eulogy, praising his friend and comrade:

> Marx was the best-hated and most slandered man of his age. Governments, both absolutist and republican, expelled him from their territories, whilst the bourgeoisie, both conservative and extreme-democratic, vied with each other in a campaign of vilification against him. He brushed it all to one side like cobwebs, ignored them and answered only when compelled to do so. And he died honoured, loved and mourned by millions of revolution-

ary workers from the Siberian mines over Europe and America to the coasts of California, and I make bold to say that although he had many opponents he had hardly a personal enemy. His name will live through the centuries and so also will his work.[10]

NOTES

[1] The literature on Marx and Marxism is exhaustive. Among the hundreds of biographies and memoirs, see, e.g.: Isaiah Berlin, *Karl Marx* (New York: Oxford University Press, 1948); Sydney Hook, *Toward the Understanding of Karl Marx* (New York: John Day, 1933); David McLellan, *Karl Marx, His Life and Thought* (New York: Harper, 1973); Franz Mehring, *Karl Marx* (1918), trans. by Edward Fitzgerald (London: Allen & Unwin, 1936); Leopold Schwartzschild, *Karl Marx: The Red Prussian* (1947); Julius Carlebach, *Karl Marx and the Radical Critique of Judaism* (London: Routledge and Kegan Paul, 1978); and David McLellan, *Marx before Marxism* (New York: Harper & Row, 1970).

[2] Marx, *Selected Essays*, trans. H.J. Stenning (New York: International Publishers, 1926), 12.

[3] Marx, *On the Jewish Question* (1844), in *Selected Essays*, 88.

[4] Schwartzschild, *Karl Marx*, 250.

[5] Marx, *Capital*, vol. I, ed. F. Engels, (New York: International Publishers, 1967)

[6] Lenin, *The Teachings of Karl Marx* (New York: 1930), 10.

[7] John Lewis, *The Life and Teaching of Karl Marx* (London: International Publishers, 1965), 185.

[8] Lewis, *The Life and Teaching of Karl Marx*, 88.

[9] Quoted in Schwartzschild, *Karl Marx: The Red Prussian*, 200.

[10]Mehring, *Karl Marx*, 532.

IV: SCIENCE AND MEDICINE

If there is one field in which German Jews have been particularly outstanding, it would be science and medicine. Already during the medieval period, Jewish doctors were highly esteemed and much in demand at the royal courts. And after the emancipation of the German Jews in the nineteenth century, many of the leading medical authorities were either Jews or men of Jewish origin. In fact, their number far exceeded their proportion in the total population, especially in the big cities, notably Berlin, where half of all the men and women engaged in medicine were of Jewish origin.

Even more striking has been the presence of Jews in the natural sciences and mathematics. This is most apparent in the number of German Jews who have received the Nobel prize.[1] And if one were to add to their numbers the Nobel prize-winners who are the offspring of mixed Jewish, non-Jewish marriages, such as the physicists Heinrich R. Hertz (after whom, the term "hertz") and Max Born, the ranks of such distinguished scientists would be even greater. As well as playing a leading role in the German universities, Jews occupied many important positions in research institutes of science and medicine and have made significant contributions in applied science in work for the leading industrial and chemical companies.

Among the most distinguished Jewish doctors of medicine, was Paul Ehrlich (born in Strehlau, 1834, died in Frankfurt, 1915). One of the most outstanding bacteriologists and biochemists of all time, Ehrlich was a pioneer in chemotherapy and the inventor of salvarsan for the treatment of syphilis. He had a brilliant career, first as head of the Institute for Serum Research in Steglitz, near Berlin, and later as the director of the Institute for Experimental Therapy in Frankfurt. In 1903, he became the first medical man since Rudolf Virchow to receive the Great Gold Medal for Science. In 1908, he was awarded the Nobel Prize in Physiology and Medicine. His contributions to hematology, cellular pathology, and the study of cancer opened up whole new areas of research and knowledge. As a Jew, he was sympathetic to the Zionist cause and was one of the founders of the Nordau Institute, which became the forerunner of Hebrew University in Jerusalem.

In the field of biology, the earliest German Jewish pioneer was Nathaniel Pringsheim (born in Wziesko,

Upper Silesia, 1823, died in Berlin, 1894). He began his career at Berlin University where he became a lecturer in 1851. Five years later, he was elected to the Berlin Academy of Science. From Berlin University, he moved to Jena in 1864 where he was professor of botany. At Jena, he found the Institute of Plant Physiology and pioneered the study of algae. His research resulted in important discoveries in the morphology and physiology of plants, most notably in plant reproduction and evolution. He also founded the German Botanical Society which he served as president, and he was the editor of *Jahrbücher für wissenschaftliche Botanik* ("Annals of Scientific Botany").

German Jewish contributions to chemistry are also impressive. Fritz Haber (born in Breslau, 1868, died in Switzerland, 1934) has already been mentioned in connection with his contribution to the German war effort at the Kaiser Wilhelm Institute (see introduction). His career began at Karlsruhe, where he was professor of physical chemistry. He went on to head the chemical division of the Kaiser Wilhelm Institute, and received the Nobel Prize in Chemistry in 1918. His most distinguished colleague was Richard Willstätter (born in Karlsruhe, 1872, died in Locarno, 1942). In 1915, during his tenure as professor at the Kaiser Wilhelm Institute, he was awarded the Nobel Prize in Chemistry. The following year, he accepted a position as professor and head of the department of organic chemistry at the University of Munich. His studies of the chemistry of life and the process of growth in plants have

ALBERT EINSTEIN

been honored by scientific organizations in France, England, and the United States. Both he and Haber fled Nazi Germany for Switzerland.

The list of German Jewish physicists is also long. Among the most outstanding is James Franck (born in Hamburg, 1882, died in Durham, North Carolina, 1964). After studying in Heidelberg and Berlin, he was appointed to Berlin University where he became a professor of physics in 1915. From there, he moved to Göttingen in 1920 to head the Physics Institute. Together with Gustav Hertz, he received the Nobel Prize for Physics in 1925. Like Haber and Willstätter, he was forced to flee Germany after the Nazis came to power. He emigrated to the United States, where he taught at Johns Hopkins University from 1935 to 1938, and then at the University of Chicago.

By far the most notable German Jewish scientist, and one of the most celebrated German Jews of the twentieth century, is Albert Einstein.[2] Although his fame rests largely on his theoretical physics, he became a well-known, beloved figure to scientists and laymen alike. His kind face, framed by an aureole of white hair, is as familiar to almost everyone as that of today's popular politician or movie star. Photographs and paintings of him have been reproduced in newspapers, magazines, and films throughout the world, and his observations, not only on physics but on life and civilization in general, have been widely quoted. His book on relativity, despite its abstract and theoretical nature, became a

97

bestseller in many countries. When Riverside Church in New York City adorned its façade with the bas-reliefs of statesmen, philosophers, and saints from different epochs, it was Einstein who was chosen to represent our period—which prompted him to say that he was the only Jewish saint in history.

When Einstein's theory was confirmed in 1919 by the observations of the astronomers, Sir Joseph John Thompson, one of the fathers of modern physics, who had won the Nobel Prize in Physics in 1906, said that Einstein's work was "one of the greatest—perhaps the greatest—of achievements in the history of human thought."[3] And Max Planck, the author of quantum theory, said in May of 1933, after Hitler had come to power:

> I believe that I speak for my Academy colleagues in physics, and also for the overwhelming majority of all German physicists when I say: Mr. Einstein is not just one among many outstanding physicists; on the contrary, Mr. Einstein is the physicist through whose works published by our Academy, physics has experienced a deepening whose significance can be matched only by that of the achievements of Johannes Kepler and Isaac Newton.[4]

Indeed, Einstein is known today as the father of modern physics. His ideas revolutionized all the laws of the universe that physicists since Newton had believed to be true.

Albert Einstein was born in Ulm on March 14, 1879. Shortly after his birth, his family moved to Munich, where young Albert grew up. His family, although of old Jewish stock, was not very religious, observing neither the Jewish holidays nor the dietary laws. Although Einstein himself grew to be a deeply spiritual man, moved by the ultimate mystery of the universe, he was not a believing Jew in any traditional sense. He once said, "I cannot conceive of a personal god who would directly influence the actions of individuals, or would directly sit in judgement on creatures of his creation. I cannot do this in spite of the fact that mechanistic causality has, to a certain extent, been placed in doubt by modern science. My religiosity consists in humble admiration of the infinitely superior spirit that reveals itself in the little that we, with our weak and transitory understanding, can comprehend of reality. Morality is of the highest importance—but for us, not for God."[5] He identified with Spinoza, who had been expelled from the synagogue for his unorthodox beliefs. For Einstein, the great religious figures such as Moses, Buddha, and Jesus, along with the great philosophers, were sources of wisdom and understanding, but he could not accept the doctrines of any religion.

As a very young child, Einstein was slow in learning to talk; and when he went to school, he apparently made very little impression on his teachers or fellow students. He attended the gymnasium in Munich, and while he excelled in mathematics and science, he did poorly in languages and history. He was unpopular with his teachers because of his independence and religious temperament; and he felt a hostility which lasted his entire life toward the rigorous curriculum and harsh discipline of the German schools.

In his early teenage years, his father's business failed, and in 1894 he moved to Milan. The young Albert joined him there without bothering to finish the gymnasium. In 1895, when Einstein was sixteen, his father decided that his son should prepare for a sensible career like electrical engineering and directed him to the canton school in Aarau, Switzerland. The following year he was accepted at the Federal Institute of Technology in Zurich, where he spent four happy years and made several good friends, notably Marcel Grossman. It was also in Zurich that he met Mileva Maric who, in 1903, became his wife. It was soon after this time that he renounced his German citizenship and became a naturalized Swiss citizen.

When he graduated from the institute in 1900, Einstein hoped for an assistantship at a university which would enable him to continue his studies; but when he found that no such position was available, he took a job in 1902 as an examiner in the Swiss patent office in Bern. Although he had had no formal training for this kind of work, he soon mastered the necessary skills and became an expert at judging the feasibility of mechanical inventions and describing them for the patent records in clear and accurate prose. Now in his twenties, Einstein spent seven years working at the patent office, during which time he also studied for his doctorate at the University of Zurich, which he received in 1905. As busy as it was, he rather enjoyed this period of his life.

It was also during this time that he began to work out

his ideas in post-Newtonian physics, writing papers that were published in the *Annals of Physics*. Indeed, it was on this work that his early fame was based. Although these were only brief articles addressed to a small scholarly audience of fellow physicists, they already showed Einstein's scientific genius, and his colleagues in Switzerland and Germany began to take notice of this brilliant young man. In 1905, at the age of twenty-six, Einstein published *Electrodynamik bewegter Körper*, a paper which established his reputation at once as one of the most original and important physicists of his day and ultimately led to his Nobel Prize in Physics in 1921. Dealing with thermodynamics and statistical mechanics, the paper raised questions about photoelectrics and quantum mechanics which took physics beyond Newtonian principles of a machine-like universe and would eventually revolutionize modern physics.

The culmination of Einstein's early work, which occupied him for almost a decade, was the theory of relativity. It not only represented one of the greatest advances ever made in human thought, it completely altered the understanding of space and time. Stated in abstract, mathematical terms, and seeming to contradict common-sense observations, Einstein's work on relativity at first was comprehensible only to a few hundred physicists and mathematicians with the sort of vision that was needed to understand the epoch-making implication of the new theory. One was the famous British astronomer, Sir Arthur Eddington, who summed up its importance in these words:

> Surely then we can best indicate the revolutionary con-
> sequences of relativity by that statement that distance and
> duration, and all the physical quantities derived from
> them, do not as hitherto supposed refer to anything
> absolute in the external world, but are relative quantities
> which alter when we pass from one observer to another
> with different motion.[6]

Einstein's work resulted in the Special Theory of
Relativity, which he explained in a paper published in
1905 when Einstein was only twenty-six years old.
Over the next ten years, he expanded on his idea, and,
in 1916, arrived at the General Theory of Relativity.
The later work broadens the theory from a scientific
and philosophical system which applied to uniform
motion to one that included nonuniform motion. Among
other things, he demonstrated that material bodies produce curvature in space—which finally explained the
behavior of the planet Mercury, long a puzzle to astronomers—and gave an entirely new, revolutionary
view of the structure and life of the universe. Many of
his theoretical calculations could be confirmed by observations made only under special conditions, during
the eclipse of the sun, for example; and it would not be
until much later in the century that scientific instru-
ments accurate enough to measure certain phenomena
he theorized about would be developed.

Although Einstein's theories immediately found some
ardent champions, there were also many sceptics. Some
were so tied to the old philosophical or scientific sys-
tems that they were simply unwilling to accept his

ideas. Others may have found the theory interesting, but held back because it could not be verified. But when Eddington sent a team of astronomers to Africa and South America in 1919 to photograph the sky during an eclipse of the sun, Einstein's hypothesis that light shifts near the sun was confirmed. When this physical evidence was reported to Einstein, he telegraphed his mother to inform her, and Eddington reports that it was the greatest day of his life. Upon returning to London, Eddington gave a report to the Royal Astronomical Society in front of an audience of Britain's most distinguished scientists and philosophers. Alfred North Whitehead, the great philosopher, said of the event:

> It was my good fortune to be present at the meeting of the Royal Society in London when the Astronomer Royal for England announced that the photographic plates of the famous eclipse, as measured by his colleagues in Greenwich Observatory, had verified the prediction of Einstein that rays of light are bent as they pass in the neighborhood of the sun. The whole atmosphere of tense interest was exactly like that of a Greek drama: we were the chorus commenting on the decree of destiny as disclosed in the development of a supreme incident. There was dramatic quality in the very staging:—the traditional ceremonial, and in the background the picture of Newton to remind us that the greatest of scientific generalizations was now, after more than two centuries, to receive its first modification.[7]

With the universal recognition that this brought him, Einstein's professional career, which had had such a slow start, sped forward. In 1909, Zurich University offered him a position as adjunct assistant professor of physics, and he accepted. This was followed in 1910 by a full professorship at the German University in Prague, and in 1912 he was appointed chair for theoretical physics at his alma mater, the Federal Institute of Technology in Zurich. Two years later, when he was thirty-five, the Prussian Academy of Sciences asked him to come to Berlin as a research professor of physics and director of theoretical physics at the prestigious Kaiser Wilhelm Institute.

As an expatriated German, he was most reluctant to accept this offer, but Germany's two most eminent physicists, Max Planck and Walter Herman Nernst, went to Zurich especially to persuade him to accept, arguing that the position would enable him to devote his entire time to research under the most favorable conditions. He was permitted to retain his Swiss citizenship which, in light of the outbreak of World War I a few months later, proved providential. As Berlin was the greatest center for scientific research at this time, with several of the most outstanding men of science working there, the appointment for such a young man to the Institute was an exceedingly high honor indeed. And so Einstein, who only a decade earlier had been unable to get even an assistantship, moved to Berlin, to assume the directorship of some of the most important theoretical work in physics being done at that time.

After science, Einstein's two great passions were music and sailing. He was a proficient violinist and enjoyed playing both for himself and in company. Above all, he loved the elegance of Mozart and Bach, caring nothing for later music; even Beethoven was too emotional and individualistic for Einstein's taste. In Berlin, surrounded as it is by lakes, he was able to indulge his love of sailing.

In many ways the two decades between 1913 and 1933 represent the apogee of Einstein's life. After a divorce from Mileva, he had married his cousin Elsa Löwenthal who, in contrast to his first wife, was no intellectual and knew nothing about physics; but she took care of him in an unpretentious, motherly way. His fame—especially after the British astronomers had confirmed the validity of his theories—reached dizzying heights. No other scientist, before or since, has enjoyed the popularity which Einstein attained during the 1920s. The image he projected as a brilliant scientist who was also a naïve, simple human being, had a tremendous appeal for all kinds of people—from the king and queen of Belgium, who became close personal friends, to the man in the street who saw him as the very archetype of the absent-minded professor.

As a lecturer, Einstein was now in demand all over the world. He gave talks on his relativity theory in England, France, Holland, Belgium, Austria, and Switzerland; he made a triumphant lecture tour in the United States, where president Harding received him in the White House; and on a tour of the Far East, he was welcomed in Japan by the entire scientific community as well as by members of the imperial family.

In spite of all this renown, and perhaps only partly

because of it, he encountered serious difficulties during these years. The outbreak of war shortly after he settled in Berlin presented great problems to him as a lifelong pacifist. Passionately opposed to militarism and to extreme nationalism, Einstein was clearly unsympathetic to the German war effort, and said so. Accusations that he lacked loyalty to his native country followed and his wife and children went to Switzerland; but he remained in the German capital, working for peace and a united Europe with Romain Rolland and other pacifists.

With the end of the war and the establishment of the Weimar Republic, everything changed, for Einstein was now hailed as a great German scientist and he was also instrumental in re-establishing cordial relations with the scientific communities in the former enemy countries. He even resumed his German citizenship, although he continued to hold his Swiss citizenship as well. But as a Jew, a pacifist, a socialist, and an internationalist, he also aroused a great deal of resentment among anti-Semitic and nationalist circles who saw him as the embodiment of everything they hated most. These sentiments were especially strong among university students and even affected the universities' administrations. From 1929, all during the Great Depression, such sentiments grew even stronger, leading to Hitler's coming to power in January, 1933. Einstein, who had seen this coming for some time, left Germany at once, never to return.

Although he was a native of Germany and a natural-

106

ized Swiss citizen, Einstein, unlike most German Jews, had never felt himself to be wholly part of either country. But in spite of the fact that he did not observe traditional Judaism, he thought of himself as first and foremost a Jew. Sympathetic to the Zionist cause, he had gone to America in the company of Chaim Weizman, the first president of Israel, to raise money for Hebrew University in Jerusalem. Like Buber, he envisaged a Jewish community in Palestine which would be a center of Jewish intellectual and cultural life. As he said in his Jewish homeland address given in London:

> The Jewish people—free from petty chauvinism and the evils of European nationalism, living peacefully side by side with the Arabs, who enjoy equal rights—should be enabled to lead its national life in its ancestral homeland, so that it may again assume a dominant role in the civilization of the world.[8]

For Einstein, the civilization of German Jews and their accommodation to German culture had been a mixed blessing, and he did not hesitate to criticize the losses of national consciousness and dignity that were its price. He accused German Jews of having become fat and lax and losing a sense of the Jewish community. As he said in the same talk in London:

> The finest elements of the human soul can only flourish in the fertile soil of the community. How doubly great, therefore, is the moral danger of the Jew who has lost his kinship with his own group and whom the people of the nation in which he lives regards as alien! Frequently such a situation has produced a harsh and dismal egoism.[9]

107

And yet Einstein never even contemplated settling in Israel when he left Germany.

His status as a world-renowned figure gave him the opportunity to move to almost any country in the world. The most eminent academic and scientific institutions everywhere vied with each other in trying to persuade him to join them. After some deliberation, he decided to become a member of the newly established Institute of Advanced Study in Princeton, New Jersey, where he was to spend the rest of his life. Meanwhile, he had been denounced in Berlin by the Nazi authorities and formally thrown out of the Prussian Academy of Sciences, and if he had not already resigned his positions at the University and the Kaiser Wilhelm Institute, he would certainly have been dismissed from these academies, too. The Nazi authorities confiscated his property and burned his books.

In the United States, Einstein spoke out vigorously against Nazis, warning against Hitler's militaristic plans. He also tried to help Jews escape Germany before it was too late. With his deep concern for his fellow scientists, especially those who were German, Austrian, and Hungarian Jews, he used all his energy and influence to secure affidavits for those who wanted to emigrate to America and to find jobs for newly arrived refugees. He sponsored many Jewish scholars for their emigration and wrote so many letters of recommendation for others—often for people he did not even know—that in the end his letters lost much of their value. The Einstein house in Princeton was a virtual hostel. It was the first waystation for many European refugees, whom he and his wife took in while they helped them find housing and employment in the new country.

Einstein's scientific work, of course, continued. The Princeton years were devoted largely to the development of his Unified Field Theory, an ambitious project which occupied him for the rest of his life. With his deeply held belief in the harmony of nature, he hoped to evolve one overriding theory to explain all the forces which governed the universe. As Lincoln Barnett writes:

> Relativity has shaped all our concepts of space, time, gravitation, and the realities that are too remote and too vast to be perceived. The Quantum Theory has shaped all our concepts of the atom, the basic units of matter and energy, and the realities that are too elusive and too small to be perceived. Yet these two great scientific systems rest on entirely different and unrelated theoretical foundations. They do not, as it were, speak the same language. The purpose of a Unified Field Theory is to construct a bridge between them.[10]

While he never found a satisfactory solution to this ultimate puzzle, his work did have a profound influence in a very different direction—the atomic bomb. It was Einstein who made President Franklin Roosevelt aware of the unbelievable power that the new weapon would have. Fearing that the Germans were working in the same field, and knowing that Otto Hahn, Strassman, and Lise Meitner had already conducted experiments involving nuclear fission in Berlin, he urged the American government to launch the same kind of research.

The result of his urgings was the Atomic Energy Project—and, ultimately, the atomic bomb.

Although Einstein had always been a pacifist, he, like Bertrand Russell, reversed himself during World War II, for he felt that only armed forces could stop Hitler. His decision to write to President Roosevelt about atomic bombs, however, was an act which he later regretted. He was also vigorously opposed to making the hydrogen bomb, and he advocated turning over all atomic weapons to a world government. After the war, he proposed that the United States and the Soviet Union share their scientific knowledge, and he continued to promote the idea of a world federation of nations whose primary purpose would be the prevention of war. As both a scientist and a humanist-idealist, he sought universal harmony above all else. In retrospect, this political view seems rather naïve.

More down-to-earth and, in an immediate sense, effective was his assumption of the presidency of the Emergency Committee of Atomic Scientists in 1946. A number of other scientists, including the physicists Leo Szilard, Weiskopf, Hans Bethe, and chemists Harold Urey and Linus Pauling, also joined the organization. Its purpose was to make the public aware of the implications of atomic power—the devastating dangers inherent in the new weapons and the need to establish some supranational agency to control them. Einstein was one of the first to sign a declaration calling for men of science to alert all the peoples and governments of the world of the disaster which the use of atomic weapons in a new war would create. It was certainly not pure chance that, in his office, a portrait of Gandhi now hung where Newton's once had.

Einstein never extended his goodwill and understanding to his native country. His dislike of Germans and Germany, which went back to his school days in Munich and World War I, was intensified by Hitler's rise to power and the terrible events of the Holocaust. Even when his old Jewish friend James Franck asked him to sign a petition to try to rebuild Germany on a democratic basis instead of destroying the country, he brusquely refused, saying that he would agitate against it. Unlike Buber, who had returned to Germany and re-established relations with old German friends whom he knew had never supported Hitler, Einstein turned down offers from Bavarian and Prussian Academies of Sciences to make him an honorary member; and unlike Henry Kissinger, who accepted the honorary citizenship of his native city of Fürth, Einstein refused to accept a similar offer from his native city of Ulm.

On his seventieth birthday, a scientific conference was held in Princeton at which leading scholars from all over the world delivered papers and spoke in Einstein's honor. He had become a legendary, almost mythical, figure and stories about his eccentricities and his kindnesses, especially to children, abounded.

In his last years, his health deteriorated and his life was circumscribed by the orders of his doctors, who even deprived him of his beloved pipe. Eventually, he could no longer play the violin which had given him so much pleasure. After the deaths of his wife and sister — the only people he felt really close to in his old age — Einstein died, shortly after his seventy-sixth birthday, acclaimed as one of the greatest scientists who has ever lived.

NOTES

[1] For a listing of the Nobel-prize winners of Jewish origin, see the *International Jewish Encyclopedia*

[2] The array of literature about Einstein and his work includes: Philipp Frank, *Einstein, His Life and Work* (New York: Knopf, 1947); R.W. Clark, *Einstein: The Life and Times* (New York: World Publishing, 1971); B. Hoffmann and H. Dukas, *Einstein: Creator and Rebel* (London: Har-Davis, MacGibbon [1973, c1972]); H. Dukas and B. Hoffmann, eds., *Albert Einstein: The Human Side* (Princeton, NJ: Princeton University Press, 1979), the most complete biography; Lincoln Barnett, *The Universe and Dr. Einstein* (New York: New American Library, 1948), probably the best explanation of his theories for the layman; J.R.L. Highfield, *The Private Lives of Albert Einstein* (London, Boston: Faber & Faber, 1994); and Michael White, *Einstein: A Life in Science* (New York, 1994). For those with scientific/mathematical background, see Albert Einstein, *Relativity: The Special and General Theory* (1916) (New York: Crown, 1961).

[3] Quoted in Hoffmann, *Einstein, Creator and Rebel*, 132.

[4] Quoted in *Ibid*, 169.

[5] Quoted in Dukas and Hoffman, eds., *Albert Einstein, The Human Side.*

[6] Sir Arthur Eddington, *The Expanding Universe* (Cambridge: University Press, 1933) and *Space, Time and Gravitation* (New York: Cambridge University Press, 1987, c1920). Quoted in R.W. Clark: *Einstein: The Life and Times*, 93.

7 A.N. Whitehead, *Science and the Modern World* (New York: Macmillan, 1941 [c1925]), 11.

8 Einstein, *Cosmic Religion* (New York: Covici–Friede, 1931), 78.

9 *Ibid.*, 2.

10Barnett, *The Universe and Dr. Einstein*, 102.

ERICH FROMM

V: PSYCHOLOGY AND PSYCHIATRY

As a minority people living in Germany, Jews of Central European origin have made major contributions to psychiatry and psychology. They had problems concerning their identity and had to make difficult adjustments, especially when they tried to assimilate to the dominant German culture. Perhaps as a result, they developed a sensitivity to human nature and psychological problems which brought about deep insights into the human psyche. This was particularly true during the late eighteenth and early twentieth centuries, when the field of psychology was becoming established.

Because two of the greatest and most influential Jewish psychiatrists, Sigmund Freud and Alfred Adler, were Austrians, they are not included in this discussion; but German Jews also played a central role in the

115

development of modern psychology and psychiatry. In fact, Jews were so prominent that two of the most important contemporary schools in these fields, namely psychoanalysis and Gestalt psychology, have often been referred to as Jewish sciences. Freud's biographer, the well known English psychoanalyst Ernst Jones, frequently said that, when he attended meetings of psychoanalysts, he realized that he was the only "goy" in the room.

Among the first major German Jewish psychiatrists was Emil Kraepelin (born in Neustrelitz, 1856, died in Munich, 1926). He was a student of Wilhelm Wundt, the great physiologist and psychologist who founded experimental psychology. At a time when few Jews were appointed to prominent academic posts, Kraepelin became professor of psychiatry at the University of Dorpat in Heidelberg and at the University of Munich. His classification of mental illnesses and abnormal states, their nomenclature and diagnostic schemes, are still being used today. Highly regarded both as a teacher and an author, he studied dementia precox (schizophrenia) and manic depression and defined their characteristics, which led to new insights into the nature of these diseases. He was also a pioneer in experimental psychology as well as the study of the influence of fatigue and alcohol on mental facilities.

Of the German Jewish psychiatrists who belonged to the psychoanalytic school, the most significant was Karl Abraham (born in Bremen, 1877, died in Berlin, 1925). He took his medical degree in Freiburg and then went

116

to Berlin, where he worked at the municipal mental hospital for seven years, when he began to work in private practice. Founder of the Berlin Psychoanalytical Society and a member of Freud's inner circle, Abraham made numerous contributions to psychoanalytic theory. He found, for example, that biology dictates specific sequences in the development of the libido, and that adult personality can be understood in terms of fixation at a particular stage of one's psychosexual development. He also studied manic depressives and distinguished between two types, one that is basically biological and the other, psychotic.

A more conventional psychologist was William Stern (born in Berlin, 1871, died in Durham, North Carolina, 1938). In Germany, he had been a professor of psychology, first in Breslau and then in Hamburg, but he was dismissed in 1933 and emigrated to the United States. His particular interest was child psychology, and he wrote the classic study on how to assess the gifts and intelligence of children and young people. Stern wrote extensively in this field. His most ambitious work is a three-volume study entitled *Person und Sache* in which he explored the differences between objects and people, including a discussion of the role of family, ethnicity, and human character in psychological development.

Among Gestalt psychologists, the most influential was Kurt Koffka (born in Berlin, 1886, died in Northhampton, Massachusetts, 1941). He received his Ph.D. from Berlin University in 1908 and was a professor of psychology at Giessen University from 1918 to

117

1927, when he left Germany. In 1928 he moved to the United States and was a research fellow and, later, a distinguished professor at Smith College. In Germany, he founded the journal *Psychologische Forschung*, which he edited from 1922 to 1935. In America, he edited the *Smith Studies in Psychology*. The most important of his writings are *The Growth of the Mind* (1924) and *Principles of Gestalt Psychology* (1935), both of which were translated into many languages.

Among the most influential of psychoanalysts since Freud was Erich Fromm, a famous but somewhat controversial figure, at least among his colleagues.[1] A prolific author in German, English, and Spanish, he wrote not only on psychology and psychiatry, but on philosophy, sociology, politics, and ethics as well, and exerted a powerful influence on contemporary thought. His best known book, *The Art of Loving* (1956), was translated into twenty-eight languages and has sold millions of copies. Since his death in 1980, his memory and influence have been kept alive by the International Erich Fromm Society based in Tübingen, the location of the Fromm Archives.

Erich Fromm was born in 1900 in Frankfurt. His father, a businessman, was descended from Orthodox rabbis. In speaking of his childhood many years later, Fromm said, "I was an only child, and I had very neurotic parents. I was probably a rather unbearably neurotic child. But very early in life I became aware of the irrationalities of human behavior. Perhaps the most decisive event in my youth was the beginning of the First World War in 1914. I was fourteen years old then, and was living in Germany. It was not long after the war started that the anti-British hysteria began to impress me."[2] As a youth, Fromm adhered to the Jewish traditions of his home and was a student of the Old Testament. His favorite authors were the Old Testament prophets, particularly Isaiah, Hosea, and Amos. At thirteen, he was introduced to the Talmud and studied Jewish mysticism and Hasidism. Although he later gave up all connections with organized Judaism, there can be no question that his early religious upbringing continued to influence his thinking throughout his life.

Fromm began his academic studies in 1918 and received his doctorate from the University of Heidelberg in 1922 with the thesis dissertation, *The Jewish Law, A Contribution to the Sociology of the Judaism of the Diaspora*. Although he had given up Judaism as a religion, he wrote several essays on Jewish topics for *Imago*, the official journal of the Psychoanalytical Society, and a book on the Old Testament and its tradition titled, *You Shall Be As Gods*. His early writings already showed the breadth of interest which was to characterize his later work.

Upon encountering Freud's teachings, he decided to become a psychoanalyst and spent six years being trained in this field. In 1926, he married Frieda Reichman, a fellow analyst, and three years later became a member of the Berlin Psychoanalytical Society. From 1929 to 1932, he was a lecturer at the Psychoanalytic Institute

119

in Frankfurt and at the University of Frankfurt. He practiced and taught orthodox Freudian psychoanalysis for several years, but he later broke with Freud and developed his own ideas. During these early years, when Fromm was still living in Germany, he published a number of articles in the journals and magazines of the psychoanalytical movement, as well as another book, *The Development of the Dogma of Christ*.

As a Jew and a socialist, he was immediately discharged from his lecture posts when the Nazis came to power, but he continued to write in German for several years, although his articles were now published in Paris, in *Zeitschrift für Sozialforschung*. Most of these writings dealt with psychoanalytical themes, but he was already interested in the ideas of Briffault and Johann Bachofen dealing with matriarchy in early societies. During this time, Fromm lived in Switzerland until he emigrated to the United States in 1934. It was not until 1939, after the outbreak of World War II when all contact with Europe was cut off, that he began to write in English, the language in which most of his major works appeared.

Fromm settled in New York and from 1934 through 1939 was associated with the International Institute of Social Research. At first he had some difficulties getting a faculty appointment at a major university. For the academic year 1940-41, he was a guest lecturer at Columbia University and then he received a professorship at Bennington College in Vermont in 1941. That same year, he published his first major book in English,

Escape from Freedom. It was during this time, too, that he divorced his first wife and married Henny Gurland, who died in 1952. The following year, he married Annis Freeman, who was his companion for the rest of his life.

Prior to the publication of *Escape from Freedom,* Fromm had been only one of many German and Austrian refugee scholars interested in psychoanalytical theory; but this book, written when he was forty, made him famous in America, and indeed, is still one of his most widely read works. The book also represented an important stage in his own intellectual development, for it demonstrated that he had broken with traditional Freudian psychoanalysis by placing far more emphasis on social forces, philosophy, religion, class structure, and economics than Freud had ever done. As he said in his dialogue with R.I. Evans, "Freud derived his typology primarily from biological elements, whereas I derive mine principally from behaviors considered in a societal context.[3]

In the forward to *Escape from Freedom*, Fromm describes the book as a character study of modern man which is based in the interaction of psychological and sociological factors that influence behavior. While others had analyzed the downfall of the Weimar Republic and the rise of Hitler from political and economic perspectives, Fromm as a psychoanalyst wanted to show the psychological roots of the appeal of Fascism. According to him, it is the alienation of modern man, his feelings of helplessness and insignificance, which make

121

him want to identify with some great leader or cause in order to give meaning to his life. This idea was first explored by the nineteenth-century Danish philosopher Søren Kierkegard who, in Fromm's words:

> describes the helpless individual torn and tormented by doubts, overwhelmed by the feelings of aloneness and insignificance. Nietzsche visualizes the approaching nihilism which was to become manifest in Nazism and paints a picture of a 'superman' as the negation of the insignificant, directionless individual he saw in reality. The theme of the powerless man has found a most precise expression in Franz Kafka's work. In his *Castle* he describes the man who wants to get in touch with the mysterious inhabitants of a castle, who are supposed to tell him what to do and show him his place in the world. All his life consists in his frantic effort to get in touch with them, but he never succeeds and is left alone with a sense of utter futility and helplessness.[4]

Fromm saw in this desire to give up one's freedom and follow a leader a masochistic element, which he believed lay at the human root of Fascism and Nazism.

Reviewing the political developments in Germany just prior to Hitler's seizing power, he explains how such a demagogue was able to mesmerize the German people. He saw the lower middle class as the mainstay of the Nazi movement: "For them, the Nazi ideology, its spirit of blind obedience to a leader and of hatred against racial and political minorities, its craving for conquest and domination, its exaltation of the German people and the Nordic Race had a tremendous emo

122

tional appeal.[5] Hitler's spellbinding oratory, with its intensity and fanaticism, struck a responsive chord in them, and he became their perfect spokesman. Ultimately, Fromm said, the sadism and masochism in the relationship between the führer and the masses fulfilled a deep psychological need.

The 1940s were a busy period for Erich Fromm. He lectured at many places, most notably the American Institute of Psychoanalysis and Yale University, and wrote numerous articles and no fewer than three books. The most important of these new books was *Man for Himself* (1947). Its opening pages quote from Buddha, Lao-tzu, Plato, Hosea, and Spinoza, indicating the kind of thinkers he was turning to. As he says in the foreword, "This book is in many respects a continuation of *Escape from Freedom*, in which I attempted to analyze modern man's escape from himself and from his freedom; in this book I discuss the problem of ethics, of norms and values leading to the realization of man's self and of his potentialities."[6]

Fromm's thought was firmly grounded in reason and humanistic ethics. Although he acknowledged the great contribution that Freud and psychoanalysis had made to the understanding of human nature with its subconscious desires and fears, he deplored the moral relativism of psychoanalysis and its divorce from ethics and philosophy. He believed that we should look at man in his totality. Moral values, Fromm wrote, are based upon inherently human qualities, and denying these leads to mental, emotional, and spiritual disintegration. In its preoccupation with success, money, and prestige, modern society neglects what is most important, namely the art of living. The science of man, he says, "rests upon the premise that its object, man, exists and that there is a human nature characteristic of the human species."[7] Although acknowledging that character is influenced by environmental and social forces, *Man for Himself* maintains that there are inherently different types of human character; nevertheless, moral values can and should be applied to all people. Fromm's basic position was that of a humanist who believed that people are capable of distinguishing what is good from what is bad, and he rejected the notion that man is innately evil.

His lectures at Yale were published in 1950 under the title *Psychoanalysis and Religion*. In them, we can see the lasting influence of his early training in Orthodox Judaism. Now, however, along with the Old Testament prophets whom he had admired as a young man, he also revered Spinoza, Buddha, and the great Christian mystics, especially Meister Eckhart. For him, they all had deep spiritual insights that could help guide modern man.

The following year, Fromm's next major book, *The Forgotten Language*, was published. In it, he reviews the various theories about the meaning of dreams, starting with the symbolism in the Old Testament and Greek mythology, and going on to discuss the ideas of Freud and C.G. Jung. He sees dreams as a symbolic language in which an individual's true self is revealed. While basing his discussion to a large extent on Freud's theory of dreams—a debt which he freely acknowledges—he differs from Freud's conviction that all dreams must be subconscious wishes. This work is also important for its insistence that the position of women must be reevaluated in psychoanalysis, because Freud was too preoccupied with men. Fromm refers back to the Swiss anthropologist Bachofen, who lived a generation before Freud in his idea of a great mother goddess who was the original deity, replaced only later by a male god:

> The rule of the great Mother is challenged by the male sons. But how can they win when they are inferior to women in one essential aspect? Women have the gift of natural creation, they can bear children. Men are sterile in this respect... Quite in contrast to Freud's assumption that the 'penis envy' is a natural phenomenon in the constitution of the woman's psyche, there are good reasons for assuming that before male supremacy there was a 'pregnancy envy' in the man, which even today can be found in numerous cases.[8]

According to Fromm, the male, unable to compete with female creativity, produces words, thoughts, and works of art.

After ten years at Bennington College, Fromm became a professor of psychoanalysis at the National University of Mexico in 1951 and director of the Institute of Psychoanalysis, a position he occupied until his retirement in 1965. In 1957, he was appointed professor at Michigan State University, and in 1961, at New York University. He was also a visiting scholar and lecturer at various academic institutions, notably the William Alanson White Institute of Psychiatry in Washington, D.C.

During his years in Mexico, his most outstanding publication was *The Art of Loving*, an immensely popular book which brought him renown throughout the world. In this work, he sees the ability to love as the most important thing in life. What he means by "love" is neither romantic love nor the *ars amandi* which teaches the proper technique of sexual intercourse, but the love of one's fellow men:

> Individual love cannot be attained without the capacity to love one's neighbor, without true humility, courage, faith and discipline. In a culture in which these qualities are rare, the attainment of the capacity to love must remain a rare achievement or—anyone can ask himself how many truly loving persons he has known.[9]

He goes on to discuss forms of love—brotherly love, maternal love, erotic love, self love, and love of God—and shows that love is a difficult art which can be mastered only with skill and concentration. For Fromm, our ability to love is what makes us truly human. Love, he cautions, should not be confused with sentimentality. It should reach into the depth of one's being, he writes, for only when one loves oneself, one's fellow men, and God, can humankind redeem itself in a world which has lost all true humanity and religious faith.

In the 1960s and into the 1970s, Fromm was at the very height of both his fame and productivity as a writer. His interests became more and more focused on religion, morality, and politics. In 1960, he published *Zen and Psychoanalysis*, which he had written with the famous Zen master Daisetzu Suzuki; and in 1961, *May Man Prevail?*, which delved into world politics. Despairing of a world filled with hatred, divided by the cold war, and facing the possibility of annihilation, Fromm took up socialist politics. He became editor of the *Socialist Humanist*, wrote a socialist manifesto and a program entitled "Let Man Prevail," contributed an article to the National Committee for a Sane Nuclear Policy, and produced an essay entitled "Der Friede, Idee und Verwirklichung" ("Peace, Idea, and Reality") for a Heidelberg *Festschrift* for Adolf Leschnitzer. Writing in English, German, and Spanish, Fromm cried out to his fellow mortals to let reason and love prevail over insanity and hatred. Over and over, he questioned why, if we still loved life and human beings, did we show such destructive behavior. What would our future be like if we did not change? he asked. Some of his writings in this period were books brought out by major publishers, others were essays which appeared in specialized, scholarly journals, and still others were articles in popular magazines like *Saturday Review* and *Newsweek*. For Time-Life Books, he wrote an essay, "On the Sources of Human Destructiveness," and for the Friends Service Committee, "War Within Man." As a socialist and humanist, he lamented the folly and cruelty of mankind but his writings were never without hope that man's moral nature would eventually prevail.

Of his writings during this period, probably the two

most important books are *Beyond the Chains of Illusion*, published in 1962, and *To Have and To Be*, which came out in 1976. The first is Fromm's assessment of Marx and Freud, the two men whose ideas had the greatest influence on him—in fact, it might be said that Fromm's own thought represents a kind of synthesis of their ideas. While his early writings owe a considerable debt to Freud, Fromm had also become interested in Marx during the 1930s, especially while he was connected with the Frankfurt Schule, which had gathered around Max Horkheimer. Under this influence, he had begun to feel that Freud had neglected the social basis of man's actions; but at the same time he thought that Marx had not made enough allowance for the psychological factors that influence human thought and action.

But it was Freud who continued to haunt him. In his last book, *Greatness and Limitations of Freud's Thought* (1979), Fromm's fundamental disagreement with Freud is most apparent in the preface, where he quotes St. John's remark, "And the truth shall make you free," as Freud's basic insight; but then he adds; "Indeed, the idea that the truth saves and heals is an old insight which the great Masters of Living have proclaimed—nobody perhaps with such radicalism and clarity as the Buddha, yet it is a thought common to Judaism and Christianity, to Socrates, Spinoza, Hegel, and Marx."[10]

To Have and To Be is in many ways Fromm's testament in which for the last time he summarized his deeply held convictions about the human dilemma and his criticism of contemporary society. As he sees it, the great fault of the modern Western world is its overriding concern with material wealth, consumption, status, knowledge, and power—all detrimental to our mental health and humanity. What should concern us, he writes, is our being instead of our goods. Medieval society, with its rejection of materialism, was, for him, more desirable than the modern world of plenty. A whole section of this book deals with Meister Eckhart, the great thirteenth-century Christian mystic whose religious and moral values he admired. He asks if the Western world is still really Christian, and he calls for a new man and a new society in which people can live fulfilling and meaningful lives.

For Erich Fromm, the man who best exemplified the highest moral values was Albert Schweitzer, about whom he wrote an essay on the occasion of Schweitzer's hundredth birthday in 1975. By this time, Fromm himself already had retired to Muralto in Switzerland, where he died at the age of eighty in 1980.

NOTES

[1] Fromm's complete works are collected in an edition of 10 vols., Ranier Funk, ed. There is also an exhaustive literature about Fromm and his ideas. See, for example, Rainer Funk, *Erich Fromm: The Courage to Be Human* (New York: Continuum, 1982); and John H. Schar, *Escape from Authority* (New York: Basic Books, 1961).

[2] Quoted in Richard I. Evans, *Dialogue with Erich Fromm* (New York: Harper & Row, 1966), 56-57.

[3] Evans, 11.

[4] Fromm, *Escape from Freedom* (New York: Farrar & Rinehart, 1941),133.

[5] *Ibid.*, 211.

[6] Fromm, *Man for Himself* (New York: Rinehart, 1947)

[7] *Ibid.*, 20.

[8] Fromm, *The Forgotten Language* (New York: Rinehart, 1951), 233.

[9] Fromm, *The Art of Loving* (New York: Harper, 1956), xix.

[10] Fromm, *Greatness and Limitations of Freud's Thought* (New York: Harper & Row, 1980), ix.

VI: BUSINESS

From the very beginning, German Jews were active in some type of business, be it as small as peddlers, traders, merchants, moneylenders, or bankers. In medieval Germany, when Jews were barred from most professions, they were encouraged to go into moneylending because Christians were forbidden to take interest. While this benefitted Jews economically, and made some richer than most of their Christian neighbors, it also gave rise to the age-old image of the Jewish money lender who exploited others, a stereotype exemplified in Shakespeare's *The Merchant of Venice* with the character of Shylock, as well as in many renditions of the unscrupulous Jew in German literature and folklore. No doubt this image was one of the factors which contributed to the early anti-Jewish sentiment in Germany that in turn led to modern anti-Semitism and the persecution of the Jews during the Nazi period.

The earliest account of Jewish merchants in Germany goes back to the seventh century and the Carolingian period. There are also many medieval reports of Jewish businessmen and moneylenders in the great cities of the Rhineland who had an essential role in the economic life of the time. But it was not until the seventeenth and eighteenth centuries, during the age of absolutism, that Jews became the financiers and advisors of many German princes. The most successful and notorious of these so-called *Finanz Juden* was Joseph Oppenheimer, better known as Jud Süss (born in Heidelberg, 1692, died in Stuttgart, 1738). A brilliant man, Oppenheimer achieved a position of unprecedented power while in the service of the Duke of Württemberg. The duke, an extravagant man, turned the administration of all his financial affairs over to Oppenheimer. The duke's income came from state monopolies and heavy taxes, which Oppenheimer was also in charge of collecting; so these became known as Jew taxes and aroused great resentment among the people. At the same time, Jud Süss lived in luxury and boasted of his influence on the duke, all of which made him so hated that, when the duke died, he was put on trial and eventually executed.

Among the nineteenth-century German Jewish financiers, the most remarkable was Gerson von Bleichroeder (born in Berlin, 1822, died in Berlin, 1893). Under his management, the Bleichroeder banking house—which had been founded by his father and was associated with the Rothschilds—became one of the leading financial institutions in Germany. He also became financial advisor to Otto von Bismark, the court banker of Emperor William I, and a major financier of the railroads. More important, he financed state loans for Prussia during the wars against Austria and France. After the defeat of France, Bleichroeder was present at the peace conference and set the amount of indemnity France was to pay. As a close personal friend of Bismark's, he had an enormous influence on the financial affairs of government. The first unconverted Jew to be elevated to the hereditary Prussian nobility, he was also active in Jewish affairs, contributing generously to charities and intervening on behalf of the oppressed Jews in the Balkans.

During the early twentieth century, many outstanding businessmen, merchants, factory owners, and bankers were Jews or of Jewish origin. The most spectacular was probably Albert Ballin (born in Hamburg, 1857, died in Hamburg, 1918). The son of a small shipowner, he started his career as an apprentice in the English Carr Line where he rose rapidly, first becoming the chief passenger agent and then, when the company was taken over by the Hamburg-America line, its general director. Under Ballin's management, the company became the biggest shipping line in Germany and one of the largest in the world. He established fast steamer service between Hamburg and New York and was the first to introduce passenger cruises. A skillful politician as well as a good businessman, Ballin was often consulted by

Emperor William II, who bestowed on him the Royal Order Second Class. An extreme patriot, Ballin was so upset by the defeat of Germany in World War I, along with the destruction of his shipping fleet, that he killed himself in 1918. He was sixty-one.

An almost exact contemporary was the enterprising Berlin businessman Oskar Tietz (born in Birnbaum, 1858, died in Berlin, 1923). With his uncles Hermann and Leonard Tietz, he established a chain of department stores. Based on American business methods, the Tietze stores became the most successful business venture in all of Germany. In Berlin alone, there were no fewer than ten Tietze stores, including the flagship store, an impressive building occupying an entire city block and crowned by a huge glass globe. The stores were famous for their food sections which offered a variety and quality of goods unequaled in any other department store. It was in these stores where the tomato and many exotic foreign fruits were introduced to the Berlin public. The Tietzes were also active in philanthropy and were prominent figures in the life of the capital.

The very name Rothschild is a symbol of riches and power. Unlike Bleichroeder, Ballin, and the Tietzes, whose influence was restricted to Germany and lasted only during their lifetime, the Rothschilds dominated the financial markets for several generations and have preserved their wealth to this day. It would not be an exaggeration to say that no other European family has ever accumulated such wealth and exerted such power.

134

While the Rothschilds were certainly admired, they were also objects of German, anti-Jewish sentiment; the family was often accused of employing unscrupulous business practices and financing both sides in European wars.

How famous the Rothschilds were and still are is best illustrated by the copious literature in German, French, and English that has grown up around the family. Several books about them were published as early as the nineteenth century, notably Friedrich Steinmann's *Das Haus Rothschild* (1858) and Eduard Demarchy's *Les Rothschilds*, which came out in Paris in 1896. In the twentieth century, long after the death of the founder and his five sons, many more books have appeared dealing with the Rothschilds, their financial affairs, and their family history.[1]

The founder of the House of Rothschild was Mayer (also spelled Meyer) Amschel Rothschild. He is described as a tall, impressive looking man, who wore a wig and had a small, pointed black beard. His features, judging from pictures, were of a marked Semitic type and throughout his life, he spoke a language that was a mixture of Yiddish and German.

Mayer was born in the Judengasse of Frankfurt in 1743, a small, narrow street that had been designated as the Jewish quarter in 1442. In 1760, it contained 3,000 inhabitants—about ten percent of Frankfurt's population—crammed into three hundred houses. Records show that Mayer's forebears had lived in a house with a red shield (*rot schild*), and it was this that gave the family their name. Mayer's father was a small trader; it is said that, as a boy, he often accompanied his father on his trips into the countryside to sell his wares. His father also did some small scale moneylending. While not well-to-do, the family was quite comfortable.

When Mayer was ten years old, his parents sent him to Fürth to a Yeshiva, or Jewish religious school, because they wanted him to become a rabbi, the calling of several of his ancestors. After a few months, however, it became clear that the youngster was not meant to be a scholar, and so in 1757, when he was thirteen, he was sent to the Oppenheim Bank in Hanover in order to learn the banking trade. Here, the boy made the acquaintance of General von Estorff, an ardent coin collector, and it was through him that the young Rothschild became interested in numismatics. He would then later serve the general as an agent in connection with his coin collection. When Mayer's father died, leaving him a small inheritance, he returned to Frankfurt and took over his father's business.

Once established in his own business, Mayer Rothschild quickly showed his great gifts for financial affairs. He specialized in money changing and dealing in rare coins, in which he was very successful. In the meantime, General von Estorff had left Hanover and joined the court of Prince William, landgrave of Hesse-cassel, the grandson of the English king George III, and the son-in-law of the Danish king, Frederick V. It was through doing business with the prince, who was an astute businessman and coin collector, that Mayer Rothschild

MAYER AMSCHEL ROTHSCHILD

made his fortune. By offering Prince William coins at very low prices and lending him money on favorable terms, Rothschild endeared himself to his patron and was awarded the title of Crown Agent in 1769. Over the course of the following year, he married the seventeen-year-old Gutle Schnapper, the daughter of one of the wealthiest merchants in the Judengasse, bought a house in which he set up a money exchange, and published a catalogue of antique coins which he sent to the prince and other collectors. Both his marriage and his business flourished; he and Gutle had ten children, five boys and five girls.

During the 1770s and 1780s, Mayer Rothschild received an even larger part of the prince's business through his close connection with William's treasurer, Carl Friedrich Buderus, especially in regard to money changing and the discounting of foreign money orders. Because his dealings were fair and he had a keen eye for profitable opportunities, both his reputation and wealth increased, and he was able to buy a fine town house in which he installed both his business and his family. Aided by his five sons, who also showed a talent for business at an early age, he became a rich man. It has been estimated that, by 1790, his yearly income was between two and three thousand guilders, which was about the same income of well-to-do non-Jewish families in Frankfurt at the time.

The most dramatic event of these years was the French Revolution, which endangered the thrones of the German princes and led to a series of wars between

France and Austria, England, and some of the German states. Although Frankfurt was twice occupied by French forces, the war benefitted the economy of the city, especially during the time when Amsterdam, its chief rival, fell to the French and its trade with England, Austria, and Germany was cut off. By now, Rothschild, no longer limiting himself to financial affairs, dealt also in cloth, foodstuffs and wine, goods which had become scarce due to the hostilities between France and England. This trade was extremely lucrative and, as Corti points out in his excellent books on the Rothschilds, "The war profits realized at that time formed the real foundation of the enormous fortune that was later built up by the House of Rothschild."[2]

As members of a close knit Jewish family, Amschel and Solomon, the two eldest sons (born 1773 and 1774), joined their father's firm. After Mayer's death in 1812, Amschel took over the Frankfurt office, and Solomon became the head of the Vienna branch of the House of Rothschild. But the most brilliant of the five sons was Nathan (born 1777). In 1798, at the age of twenty-one, he decided to move to England to establish a new branch of the firm. He took 20,000 pounds in capital with him, the equivalent of one million guilders, of which a fifth was his own money. Although he did not know a word of English and arrived in England a complete stranger and a Jew, Nathan became the most successful of all the Rothschilds and one of the wealthiest men in England.

Nathan's younger brothers James (born 1792) and Karl (born 1788) established a branch of the Rothschild business in Paris and Naples. Thus the firm became truly international. It was this financial empire established by Mayer and his five sons that enabled the family to acquire a wealth which surpassed that of any Jewish family and, according to many historians, was the greatest fortune ever assembled. A remark made by their mother years later illustrates the immense power they wielded, for once when asked if there would be a war between the two German states, she said, "Nonsense. My boys won't give them the money."[3]

In the years between Napoleon's rise to power and the disastrous Russian campaign, the Rothschilds lent funds to the Danish king, the English crown prince, and the emperor of Austria, and became the dominant figures in the European financial world. Indeed, Mayer Rothschild drew his old patron the prince of Hesse-Cassel (now Elector William I) further into his debt by hiding the prince's assets and wisely investing his English interest payments when William was removed from his throne by Napoleon and had to flee for his life. In this enterprise as well as in bringing in contraband goods from England during the blockade of the continent, Mayer Rothschild was substantially helped by his son Nathan, both of whom further enriched themselves by the venture.

The end of Mayer Rothschild's life came on September 19, 1812. His last days were spent observing Yom Kippur, the most sacred Jewish holiday, devoted to repenting for one's sins. As a pious Jew who had always observed the holidays, the old man had fasted and spent many hours standing in the synagogue praying. That evening, he was attacked by pain and, as his condition worsened, he developed a burning fever. Realizing that death was approaching, he made a new will, bequeathing his estate to his five sons and also leaving an inheritance to his daughters. Three days later he died at the age of sixty-nine.[4]

The death of the founder of the Rothschild dynasty did not greatly affect the affairs of the firm, for the five sons, whom he had wisely placed in important commercial centers, worked closely together and established a banking house whose equal the world had never seen. Nathan first settled in Manchester, the center of the textile industry, and then moved to London. He had a highly efficient courier service which gave him access to confidential information about political and economic developments much earlier than official government sources could, and he had learned about Napoleon's defeat at Waterloo a day before it became public knowledge. After the defeat of Napoleon, London became the largest financial and trading center in the world. Having helped finance Wellington's campaign in Spain as well as lending money to the British government, Nathan emerged as one of the most powerful financiers in Britain.

He brother James followed a similar path in Paris by lending money to the Bourbons, who had been restored to the throne, and financing the French military in Spain. With his great wealth, he acquired a beautiful palace in Paris and entered into French society. In Vienna, Solomon made himself useful to the Austrian emperor by extending loans to the state through the good offices of Metternich's secretary, Friedrich von Gentz, whose favor he had courted. As a result, the Rothschilds were ennobled in 1916 and later made barons, a rare distinction for Jews at this time. The distinctions they received were not limited to the countries where they lived; the tsar of Russia, for example, awarded the Rothschild brothers the Order of Vladimir for the loans which they had advanced to the Russian government. The only one of the brothers to remain in Frankfurt was Amschel, regarded as the least gifted, but as this was the birthplace of the House of Rothschild, and as Frankfurt was halfway between Paris and Vienna, he too had an important role to play in the family business.

Although the Rothschilds associated with the most prominent figures of their day, including members of royal families, all the brothers remained loyal to their Jewish faith and married Jewish women; some of the daughters, however, married members of the English and French nobility. Their mother Gutle, who lived into her nineties, remained in the Frankfurt ghetto in the House of the Red Shield which had been their original home. Her children and grandchildren came from all over Europe to visit her there, and although she was a simple, uncultured woman, she was keenly aware of the splendid position her sons had attained.

The Rothschilds not only observed the Jewish religion, they also used their great influence to help their coreligionists whenever the opportunity arose. They were particularly interested in improving the condition of the Jews in their native city, and Amschel scored a great victory in this regard when Frankfurt abolished Jewish segregation to the ghetto in 1822, permitting Jews to live in other parts of the city. And when Karl, the brother in Naples, lent money to the Pope, he did so on the condition that the prelate help to abolish the ghetto in Rome. Solomon also worked on behalf of Jews in Austria, where they were not permitted to own houses or land; and Nathan petitioned the British House of Commons to give British Jews full citizen's rights, which French Jews had had since the revolution.

The period of greatest financial power for the Rothschilds was the first half of the nineteenth century; but with changes in the ways states conducted their financial affairs during the last half of the century, their influence began to decline. In the wake of the Italian annexation of Naples in 1860, Karl closed his branch. After Amschel's death in 1855, the Frankfurt bank was taken over by Karl's sons, but it closed its doors in 1901. The Viennese branch continued until 1938, when the last Austrian Rothschild had to buy his freedom with a huge bribe to the Nazi SS chief Heinrich Himmler, who had come to Vienna to personally negotiate the deal.

Today, Rothschild banks still exist in Paris and London, and family members are active in the financial affairs of France and England; there are English Rothschilds who are lords and French Rothschilds who are barons, but they are neither as powerful or wealthy as their forebears. Indeed, the Rothschilds today are much better known for their patronage of the arts, for their horse stables and vineyards, or as writers, entomologists, and doctors. But as it always has been, Rothschilds today continue to be among the world's greatest philanthropists.

NOTES

[1] One of the best accounts of the financial aspects of the House of Rothschild was written by Christian Berghoeffer, a business partner of the Rothschilds. See Berghoeffer, *Meyer Amschel Rothschild* (1923). For excellent accounts of the history of the family, see Egon Caeser Corti, *The Rise of the House of Rothschild* (New York: Cosmopolitan Book Corp., 1928); and *The Reign of the House of Rothschild* (New York: Cosmopolitan Book Corp., 1928). See also Virginia Cowles, *The Rothschilds: A Family of Fortune* (New York: Knopf, 1973).

[2] Corti, *The Rise of the House of Rothschild*, 22.

[3] Quoted in Cowles, *The Rothschilds*, 69.

[4] Corti, 106.

VII: POLITICS

Compared to the brilliant contributions made by German Jews in various intellectual and economic fields, the role of Jews in German politics was far less significant. Certainly no German Jew ever attained the high position Disraeli achieved in England, Leon Blum in France, or Leon Trotsky in Russia. Indeed, before the revolution of 1848, it was not possible for an unconverted Jew to be active in public life or serve in the legislature of the German states and municipalities; for while Jews had been granted citizenship, they did not enjoy full political rights until the establishment of the Empire in 1871 under William I and Bismarck.

German Jews who entered political life after 1871 mostly belonged to one of the liberal parties or to the Social Democratic Party. The former were largely from the middle class; during the Empire they joined the Progressive or the National Liberal Party and, during the years of the Weimar Republic, the Democratic Party. Social Democrats, as well as other socialists, usually were from the working class. After the establishment of the Republic in 1918, some of the more radical of these became members of the Spartacus Party and, later, the Communist Party of Germany. Because Jews were never more than one percent of the German population and were scattered all over Germany, Jewish politicians had to depend on the support of their non-Jewish neighbors if they were to be elected to any office, a support which some of them did, indeed, receive.

The first unconverted German Jew to succeed as a politician was Heinrich Simon (born in Breslau, 1805, died in exile in Switzerland, 1860). After studying law at the universities of Breslau and Berlin, he embarked upon a legal career, working as a lawyer in Berlin and serving as an assistant judge from 1834 to 1841. An energetic and courageous person, Simon killed his opponent during a duel and was given a life sentence which was commuted in 1830. He wrote a widely acclaimed book on Prussian law and, during the revolution of 1848, he was active in the Frankfurt Parliament. As one of the leaders of the Democrats, he was a member of the delegation sent to negotiate the new constitution with Frederick William IV of Prussia. A member of the National Assembly in Frankfurt, 1848-49, he represented the extreme left of the Democrats.

After the defeat of the revolution, Simon was forced to leave Germany. He settled in Switzerland where he was highly regarded as a political thinker and received an honorary Ph.D. from Zurich University.

Far more successful politicians were Ludwig Bamberger (born in Mainz, 1823, and died in Berlin, 1899) and Eduard Lasker (born in Jarotschin, Posin, 1829, and died in New York, 1884, while on a trip to the United States). Bamberger was educated in law at the universities of Giessen, Heidelberg, and Göttingen. As a young man, he took part in the 1848 revolution. Condemned to death as a rebel, he fled first to Switzerland and later to Belgium, England, and the Netherlands. However, by his thirties, he had grown more conservative. In 1853, he became a banker in Paris and achieved considerable success in finance. After the amnesty of 1866, Bamberger returned to Germany. Now he began to play an important role in liberal German politics and was elected to the German parliament, where he served from 1868 to 1893. He became known as an expert on economic affairs , and Bismark himself consulted him about business matters. One of the founders of the National Liberal Party, he was highly esteemed by his political colleagues as an advocate of free trade, an authority on tariffs and standards of currency, as well as a brilliant orator. He is perhaps best known for founding the German state bank and for his successful attempts to get German currency on the gold standard. Although Bamberger was not religious, he always stressed his Jewish heritage and fought for Jewish rights.

His close friend, the other leading Jewish liberal politician, was Eduard Lasker. He studied law in England from 1855 to 1858 and became an associate judge in Berlin. From 1865 to 1879, he was a member of the Prussian diet. In 1867, he was elected to the German parliament, where he served until 1883. Although he first belonged to the Progressive Party, he helped Bamberger found the National Liberal Party in 1866 which was responsible for liberal economic legislation. Like Bamberger, he initially supported Bismark, but broke with the chancellor over social legislation and tariff policy. In 1880, he left the National Liberals and joined the *Freisinnige*, or Free Thinking Party, a more democratic wing of the liberals. Lasker, too, was not an observant Jew but he did much on behalf of Jewish causes.

Of German Jews who were active in the Social Democratic Party, by far the most popular was Paul Singer (born in Berlin, 1844, where he also died, 1911). He and his brother established a coat factory in 1869, and although the business was a success, he retired from it in 1886 to devote himself wholly to politics. At first, he belonged to the National Liberals, but his growing concern with the plight of the working class prompted him to join the Social Democratic Party in 1878. Singer soon became one of that party's most prominent leaders, and in 1884 he was elected as a Social Democrat to the German parliament. Two years later, he was expelled from Berlin as an agitator, but the order was soon rescinded. In 1887, he was elected to the executive board of the Social Democratic Party and three years later became its chairman. A compassionate man of great human warmth, Singer was a popular figure, an easy choice to represent the German socialists at many international congresses. In 1884 he founded the first working class paper in Berlin, the *Volksblatt*, which later became *Vorwärts*.

The most famous of all German Jewish politicians was Ferdinand Lassalle, a colorful, charismatic figure whose life was cut short at the age of thirty-nine. A founder of the first German workers' political party, he was a legend in his own time, the subject of innumerable books and memoirs. Various friends wrote about their relationship with Lassalle, and his political associates published books about his contribution to the establishment of the workers' movement in Germany.[1]

Like many distinguished German Jews, Lassalle was a native of Breslau, which was a center of Jewish commerce and learning during the nineteenth century. Born as Ferdinand Lassal on April 11, 1825, he changed his name to Lassalle in Paris in 1846, presumably because it sounded more cosmopolitan and less distinctly Jewish. His father was a well-to-do merchant of no particular distinction, and his mother was a strong woman, deeply attached to her brilliant son. Although Lassalle left Breslau for a world quite different from his family's, he remained close to his parents, and they took a keen interest in his career. When he was young, he was deeply involved in his Jewishness, seeing himself as a

149

FERDINAND LASSALLE

romantic figure, a champion of the Jewish cause. At age fifteen, he wrote in his diary: "I would risk my life to free the Jews from the oppression which now burdens them."[2] But it was a cause he never actually took up, and in his later life, he came to dislike and even avoid fellow Jews.

Although he was a gifted student, the young Lassalle did not adjust well to the harsh discipline of the Prussian gymnasium in Breslau, and his teachers often found him arrogant and difficult to handle. Sensitive to his difficulties at the gymnasium, his parents sent him to a commercial school in Leipzig. But it did not take him long to decide he was not interested in business, and in 1842, at the age of seventeen, he enrolled at the university in Breslau. He continued his education at the university in Berlin, where he studied philology, history, and, above all, philosophy under Hegel. He became a young Hegelian and, like many young intellectual of the period, began to consider an academic career in philosophy, which he regarded as the queen of the sciences and Hegel as its guiding spirit.

A turning point in Lassalle's life came during the winter of 1845-46, when he spent some time in Paris doing research for a book on the Greek philosopher Heraclitus. It was here that he met the German emigré Grün, the apostle of true socialism, who introduced him to the writings of the French socialist Pierre Joseph Proudhon. He also met the poet Heinrich Heine, a fellow German Jew who was living in Paris at that time. Heine was impressed with the brilliant young man and

151

gave him an introduction to Karl August Varnhagen von Ense, the well known German poet and journalist and the husband of Rahel Levin whose Berlin salons were famous throughout Europe. Heine wrote; "My friend Herr Lassalle is a young man with remarkable intellectual gifts, with the greatest devotion to study, the widest knowledge and the keenest judgment I have so far met. He unites, to a degree that astonished me, a power of exposition, a strength of will and a practical sense of business that will, if I continue to enjoy his friendship, be of the greatest value to me."[3]

With the help of Varnhagen von Ense, Lassalle became part of the intellectual life of Berlin, where he met such distinguished figures as the naturalist Alexander von Humboldt and Prince Pückler-Muskau, the well known writer who had created a world-famous park on his estate. Handsome, brilliant, and filled with the arrogance of his own ego, the young Ferdinand lived in grand style as a protégé of the cultural elite of the Prussian capital.

In 1846, Lassalle met countess Sophie von Hatzfeldt, the daughter of Prince Franz Ludwig von Hatzfeldt who was the head of one of the richest and most influential noble families in Germany. A beautiful woman twenty years his senior, the countess flattered him with attention and soon developed an intimate relationship with him that, in one form or another, was to last for the rest of his life. Just what it consisted of has been the subject of endless speculation. By most reports, their affair was initially sexual, but there is little doubt that it later became a purely platonic relationship, with the older countess playing the role of confidant, close friend, and mother-figure. Whether or not Lassalle remained intimate with the countess, it was well known that he also had many other affairs and even proposed to several young women. All the women in his life belonged to the aristocracy; none had the slightest connection with the Jewish world from which Lassalle had come.

At the time they met, Countess Hatzfeldt was separated from her husband and engaged in a battle over her divorce settlement which involved the money she had brought into the marriage. The case dragged on for eight years of complex legal actions, intrigues, the theft of a casket, as well as adultery on the part of the count, and took up Lassalle's time and energy: he devoted himself to it "to the exclusion of all his personal, academic, and family interests."[4] Finally, in 1854, the countess was vindicated and her great fortune was restored to her. She rewarded Lassalle with a lifetime income of four thousand thaler, a substantial sum which freed him from all financial worries for the rest of his life.

During all this time and in spite of his luxurious life style and aristocratic acquaintances, Lassalle was active in politics. As with so many members of his generation, the events of the 1848 revolution had an enormous impact on him and, although he was still very young, he became one of the leading spokesmen for the republican cause. He was a collaborator on the journal *Neue Rheinische Zeitung*, which Marx edited, and was also a forceful public speaker at the political meetings of the democratic forces. In May of 1849 he was accused of inciting violence against the state but, after a spirited defense, he was freed. Shortly afterward, however, he was indicted again and this time was sentenced to six months in jail. In the speech that he delivered before the court, he described himself as a "revolutionary from principle" and gave a passionate defense of his activities, a speech which was one of the most brilliant performances of his career.

After the defeat of the revolution, Lassalle once again returned to his studies. In 1858, he completed a two-volume work on Heraclitus which established his reputation as a classical scholar. He then produced an impressive book on legal rights, called *Das System der Erworbenen Rechte* ("The System of Acquired Rights"), which was published in 1861. He also wrote a drama based on the life of the sixteenth-century German knight Franz von Sickingen. Although it was not very effective as a play, it showed his literary talent, and through the speeches of its hero and his companion Hutton, it expressed many of Lassalle's political ideas. He also wrote a pamphlet about the war between France and Austria, in which he urged Prussia to seize the opportunity to unite all the German states with the exception of Austria, a development which actually took place a decade later under Bismarck.

Because of Lassalle's revolutionary activities, it became impossible for him to live in Berlin. Forced to leave the city, he spent the decade between 1848 and

1858 with Countess Hatzfeldt in Düsseldorf. But compared to the Prussian capital, the Rhineland was too provincial for him, and he longed to return. In 1857, he succeeded in doing so dressed as a coachman; then, through his well-placed connections in the capital, notably his friend and patron Alexander von Humboldt, he succeeded in getting permission to reside in Berlin.

Lassalle settled down in a fine apartment in the Bellevue Strasse near the Tiergarten, a street of beautiful chestnut trees and elegant villas in the most fashionable part of the city. With his reputation as a scholar and his fame as a leading champion of the republican cause, he was now a full-fledged part of the literary and social circles of Berlin society. Speaking of his life there, Brandes writes:

> In his house, which was decorated with elaborate splendour, according to the ideas and conditions of that age, he enjoyed the pleasure of gathering an ever-increasing circle of highly educated, clever, and cultured men, free from prejudice, many of whom were far-famed, and of beautiful, vivacious women, in many cases celebrated for their wit and talent; and among the aristocracy of mind were to be found numerous members of the aristocracy of birth.[5]

Lassalle's character was contradictory: on the one hand, he was a bon vivant, a dandy, and an intellectual and social snob; on the other, he was a left-wing revolutionary. In a letter to Sonia Sontsev, a young lady of the Russian nobility to whom he was proposing marriage, Lassalle described himself as a radical in these words:

155

> I am a man who has devoted his whole existence to a holy
> cause, the cause of the People, absolutely and uncompro-
> misingly. That cause will triumph before the close of the
> century, but meanwhile its adherents must face the risk of
> dangers and defeats. My fortune, my freedom, my life,
> may well be in constant jeopardy.[6]

As an agitator and social activist, Lassalle looms large
in the history of the German labor movement. Like
Marx, whom he visited in London and who in turn was
Lassalle's house guest in Berlin, he was hostile to the
liberal bourgeoisie and advocated the emancipation of
the working class and its rise to power. Franz Mehring,
the official Marxist historian of the Social Democratic
Party, hails Lassalle in his *Geschichte der Deutschen
Sozialdemokratie* ("History of the German Social Democrats"), devoting a hundred fifty pages of his magnum
opus to Lassalle, his theories, his role in German politics
and his activity as an agitator, writer, and organizer.[7]

What is astonishing is that the period during which
Lassalle played such an important role in politics was
actually very brief, largely from 1862 to 1864. It was
during this time that his fame spread all over Europe as
a brilliant and courageous spokesman for the working
class. Between March 1862 and June 1864, he wrote no
fewer than twenty books and pamphlets, gave numerous public addresses—some of which were distributed
in printed form—met with the deputations of workers,
tended to several political lawsuits, carried on an enormous correspondence and, most important, founded
the General German Workers' Association. While Marx's

influence was no doubt more profound and ultimately far more widespread, the fact is that, while Marx buried himself in his research at the library of the British Museum, it was Lassalle who addressed meetings of the revolutionary workers, expounding the ideas of socialism in forceful, effective popular speeches.

Because of Lassalle's fame, he was invited by a committee of workers' societies to develop a program for the Workers Congress of 1863, and what he produced established him as the leading theorist of the German socialist movement. As he saw it, the factor that was most harmful to the proletariat was the so-called "iron law of wages," a term coined by the great early nineteenth-century English economist David Ricardo. According to the "iron law of wages," workers' pay would always tend to stay at the minimum necessary to keep them alive because any time the working class was paid more than that, its birth rate rose, so that there would be many more workers than there were jobs; and this glut of workers would push wages back down to the subsistence level again. Lassalle maintained that only by workers forming production associations with state help could this condition be ameliorated, for as long as capitalists owned the means of production, they would continue to exploit the workers, pointing to the "iron law of wages." Finally, Lassalle opposed the three-tier voting system in Prussia, which gave the aristocracy and capitalists far more weight then the middle class and the workers, and called eloquently for equal voting rights for all.

Lassalle's programs were adopted by the Worker's Congress, which met in Leipzig in June of 1863 and led to the founding of the General German Workers' Association, the forerunner of the German Social Democratic Party. Marx, who up to this time had been friendly with him and had accepted financial help from him, now broke off all relations with Lassalle. No doubt this was partly due to a personal rivalry between two very different people, both of whom wanted to control the German workers' movement; but it was also because of a fundamental disagreement on basic points of doctrine. While Marx was an internationalist who saw the revolution coming first in the most advanced industrial countries, notably France and England, Lassalle was a German nationalist who wanted Germany to become a united and powerful nation. Marx saw the class struggle as the central force in the historical dialectic of the workers' movement, while Lassalle played this down and even met with Bismarck in an attempt to gain voting rights for the workers through the intervention of the chancellor. (The correspondence between Bismarck and Lassalle, which was discovered in Berlin in 1927, shows that it was Bismarck who initiated the meetings. Later, he said that he thought Lassalle one of the most intelligent and likeable men he had ever met.)

Although the General German Workers' Association never became the mass party Lassalle had envisaged, it attracted many workers, especially in the Rhineland. He had hoped for a hundred thousand members, but the total membership never exceeded five thousand.

The largest locals were in the Rhineland cities of Barmen, Ronsdorf, Solingen, Düsseldorf, Cologne, Saxony, and Hamburg. In Berlin, the working class tended to remain loyal to the left wing of the Progressive Party.

The Prussian government kept a close watch on Lassalle's activities, considering him a revolutionary agitator who was bent on stirring up the masses and spreading discontent among the working class. When trouble arose in Solingen and workers accused of assaulting the police were sentenced to three months of hard labor, Lassalle himself was charged with inciting the violence and was sentenced in absentia to twelve months' imprisonment. As a result of his appeal, conducted with his usual ardor and oratorical skill, the sentence was reduced to six months; he found this unacceptable and appealed to the Prussian Supreme Court. All this exhausted him and affected his overall health, and he decided to take a cure, first at Bad Ems and then at Sanatorium Rigi near Bern in Switzerland.

At Rigi, Lassalle the lady's man encountered a charming young woman of his acquaintance, Helene von Dönniges, whose father was a Bavarian ambassador to Switzerland. According to her memoir, he fell madly in love with her and proposed marriage. "'We are,' he told her, 'each other's fate.'"[8] Helene responded to his declaration of love and, promising to reply to his proposal by letter, left for Bern where her family was living.

Helene's father and brother vehemently opposed the idea of her marriage to Ferdinand Lassalle. A Jew as well as a political radical, he most certainly was not "one of

159

theirs," and such a marriage, they no doubt feared, would damage the family's social position and her father's diplomatic career.

In Helene's reply to Lassalle's marriage proposal, she asked him to come to Bern and seek her family's consent. She added that if they refused to give it, she would elope with him abroad. By the time he arrived in Bern, Helene's family had absolutely forbidden her to see Lassalle again, and locked her in her bedroom. Still, Lassalle went to confront her family, in the hopes that his charm and eloquence would win them over. But they would not even see him, nor would they accept his impassioned letters.

Under the pressures of her family, Helene finally gave up what she called in her memoirs the great love of her life, and accepted the marriage proposal of a Walachian nobleman, Yanko von Rakowitza. Lassalle took this all as an outrage against his honor and challenged Helene's father and her fiancé to a duel. His challenge was accepted, and von Rakowitza fatally wounded Lassalle, thus ending the life of one of the most exceptional political and romantic figures of the nineteenth century.

The news of Lassalle's death spread like wildfire, and a huge crowd of some four thousand people attended the requiem service in the Geneva synagogue, among them the two most famous Russian revolutionary emigrés, Aleksandr Herzen and Mikhail Bakunin. Countess von Hatzfeldt had his body embalmed and displayed it in various cities of the Rhineland, where thousands of workers paid a last homage to their slain leader.

Many of his followers refused to believe that Lassalle had died in a duel over a love affair, convinced that his death had to be the result of the machinations of his political enemies. A veritable Lassalle cult grew up which the countess did everything to encourage. Even Friedrich Engels, who had disliked and disagreed with Lassalle, was moved to write, in a letter to Marx, "Whatever Lassalle may have been personally, or as a thinker or man of letters, he was undoubtedly one of the most important men in Germany." And Marx himself, writing to Countess Hatzfeldt, for whom he always had a high regard said, "I know what he was for you and what his loss will mean. But take heart over this— he died young, in triumph, like Achilles.... You are right in feeling that I, more than others, can appreciate his greatness and importance."[9]

NOTES

[1] The first book about Lassalle was published in Germany in 1881. See George Brandes, *Ferdinand Lassalle* (New York: Macmillan, 1911). Other works on Lassalle include: Eduard Bernstein, *Ferdinand Lassalle as a Social Reformer,* (St. Clair Shores, MI: Scholarly Press, 1970); Hermann Oncken, *Lasalle: eine politische Biographie*, (Stuttgart: Deutsche Verlags-Anstalt, 1920); Arnold Schirokauer, *Lassalle: The Power of Illusion and the Illusion of Power*; David Footman, *Ferdinand Lassalle: Romantic Revolutionary* (1947) (New Haven, CT: Yale University Press, 1969). See also Ferdinand J.G. Lassalle, *Gesammelte Reden und Schriften*, edited by Eduard Bernstein (Berlin: P. Cassirer, 1919-20) 12 vols. Lassalle's dramatic love life is the subject of the famous novel by George Meredith, *The Tragic Comedians.*

[2] Brandes, *Ferdinand Lassalle*, 9.

[3] Quoted in Footman, *Ferdinand Lassalle*, 49-50.

[4] *Ibid.*, 52.

[5] Brandes, 88.

[6] Quoted in Footman, 119.

[7] Franz Mehring, *Geschichte der deutschen Sozialdemokratie* (Berlin: Dietz, 1960 [c1898]).

[8] Quoted in Footman, 213.

[9] Footman, 242.

VIII: GOVERNMENT

Even after German Jews had received full citizenship rights and were able to participate in the political life of Germany, the road to high government positions remained closed to them. This was especially true in Prussia where ministers, high-ranking government officials, and diplomats were usually recruited from the nobility, and men of Jewish descent, particularly if they were unconverted, had little opportunity to rise to positions higher than councilor or judge, and then only rarely. There were a few exceptions in the more liberal states: in Baden, the finance minister from 1866 to 1891 was a Jew, Moriz Ellstädter. He established a new method of collecting taxes, which was so effective that it was imitated in Prussia and other German states.

The situation changed drastically with the establishment of the Weimar Republic in 1918. For the first time, men of Jewish descent could aspire to the highest government offices. But even then—and despite the fact that, later, Hitler and the anti-Semites would refer to the new state as the Jew Republic—there were only two Jews and three men of Jewish lineage who served at the ministerial level during the fourteen years of the Weimar Republic.[1] Furthermore, none of them served for any length of time, and only one of them was a statesman of overriding importance.

The first German Jew to achieve a position of eminence in German government was Eduard von Simson (born in Königsberg, 1810, died in Berlin, 1899). Although he belonged to an old and distinguished Jewish family, he converted in 1823 at the age of twelve. When he was eighteen, he was introduced to Goethe. In later years, he became the founder and the president of the Goethe Society. Simson studied law and became a noted jurist, serving as the first presiding judge of the German Supreme Court. His greatest success came when he was elected president of the Frankfurt National Assembly of 1848-49 and the head of the delegation that informed the king of Prussia that he had been chosen to be the emperor of Germany. Simson was president of the German parliament from 1871 to 1879, and in 1888 he was elevated to the hereditary nobility, a rare honor for anyone of Jewish descent.

Of German Jews who became prominent during the Weimar Republic, one of the most influential was Hugo Preuss (born in Berlin, 1860, died in Berlin,

1925). After studying law at Berlin University, he became a docent and, in 1906, a professor of public law at Berlin Commercial University; in years later he was its rector. The abdication of Emperor William II in 1918 led to the swift transformations of the German monarchies into republics. Even Prussia became a republic overnight, and Preuss was named secretary of the interior and then minister of the interior, the highest office any German Jew had occupied up to that time. As minister, he drew up the laws governing the elections to the new constituent assembly and was largely responsible for writing the constitution for the republic. However, in the summer of 1919 he resigned from the government in protest over the signing of the Versailles Peace Treaty whose harsh terms he opposed, although he continued his work on the German constitution, which he completed in 1921.

Another German Jew who became a minister in the Weimar government was Otto Landsberg (born in Rybnik, Upper Silesia, 1869, died in Belgium, 1940). While still a student at Berlin University, he joined the Social Democratic Party and was elected to the town council in Magdeburg. In 1912, he was elected to the German parliament. Landsberg belonged to the right wing of the party and opposed the left-wing Spartacists. He was taken hostage by his opponents, but at the last moment, he was rescued by Friedrich Ebert, president of the Weimar Republic. In 1919, Ebert appointed Landsberg minister of justice. Like Preuss, he opposed the signing of the Versailles Peace Treaty and resigned

165

from the government a short time later. In 1924, he was returned to parliament where he served until his ouster by the Nazis. Landsberg fled to Belgium, where he was killed by Nazis in 1940.

Another high-ranking German politician of Jewish origin during the Weimar years was Rudolf Hilferding (born in Vienna, 1877, died in Paris, 1941). Although he was Viennese, he spent most of his life in Germany and became a German citizen. Hilferding started out as a medical doctor but gave up this profession in order to try to help solve the economic and social problems facing the country. He settled in Berlin and, from 1907 to 1915, was a writer for the Berlin socialist newspaper *Vorwärts* and one of the leaders of the Independent Socialists. When his group joined the Majority Socialists in 1923, he became a member of the executive committee of the Social Democratic Party. He also served as minister of finance in the Stresemann cabinet of 1923 and again under Hermann Müller from 1928 to 1929. In the years from 1924 to 1933, he was a party deputee in parliament. When Hitler came to power, Hilferding returned to Vienna, then went to Prague and finally to Paris, where he was arrested by the Gestapo and put to death in 1941.

One of the most brilliant and gifted statesmen in the Weimar Republic—and, indeed in the whole of German history—was Walter Rathenau. A man of great versatility, Rathenau was an outstanding scientist, a business leader, a consultant to the government during

World War I, and a prolific author, as well as the German minister of reconstruction after the war and, from 1922, the German foreign minister. His career was spectacular by any standards, and he is still remembered today, when most of the Weimar politicians have been forgotten.[2]

Walter Rathenau was born in Berlin on September 29, 1867. His father, Emil Rathenau, had founded AEG, the German electric utility company and was one of the most successful and innovative businessmen in Berlin. His mother came from a well-to-do Frankfurt banking family. She was a Lieberman, prominent in Berlin society and related to the famous painter and etcher Max Lieberman. When Walter was born, the Rathenaus lived in relative simplicity in the north of the city but, soon after, they moved to the fashionable Tiergarten district where they maintained a villa in Victoria Strasse. His mother lived there until the day she died.

Young Walter was educated primarily in day schools and by private tutors. Literature and music were his favorite subjects, and while he was still a student, he wrote a play. Perhaps from his mother's side, he was also gifted in painting and at first considered a career in the arts. But as his father's son, he felt obliged to study mathematics, physics, and chemistry, which he did at the universities of Berlin and Strassburg. He graduated in 1889, at the age of twenty-two, with a Ph.D. dissertation on the light absorption of metals. In 1892, he invented a process for producing chlomic and alkalis by

WALTER RATHENAU

means of electrolysis. That same year, he took up the management of an electrochemical works in the small industrial town of Bitterfield where he spent the next seven years.

Rathenau joined the directorate of AEG in 1899. Three years later he also took up banking in association with the Berlin Trading Company. Having established himself as an applied scientist, an industrial manager, and a financial expert, he was made chairman of the board of AEG in 1912. On his father's death in 1915, he became its president. He was also elected to the boards of directors of many other firms, eventually holding board seats with more than a hundred companies. A life-long bachelor, Rathenau built a splendid villa in the Grunewald district of Berlin, where his neighbors included such famous contemporaries as the dramatist Gerhart Hauptmann, the musician Fritz Kreisler, the newspaper magnate Ullstein, the publisher Fischer, the journalist Maximilian Harden, and several members of the Mendelssohn family. His country house in Freienwalde had been the residence of Queen Louise and was designed by the famous neo-Classical architect Friedrich Gilly.

A lively raconteur with brilliant intellect and a forceful personality, Walter Rathenau was well received in Berlin society, a guest in the most fashionable houses and the first Jew to be accepted in the aristocratic salons of the capital. He could be found at the parties of Prince Bernard von Bülow, the German chancellor from 1900 to 1909, and he was received by Emperor William II, who found him to be an engaging, impressive individual.

The German government often consulted Rathenau over economic and industrial matters, and when World War I broke out, he was chosen to organize the supply of raw materials for the war effort. For a brief period, he functioned as a kind of economic tsar for the war ministry, directing the distribution of metals, cotton, leather, skins, flax, linen, and chemicals that were in short supply. He founded several companies to undertake this effort, and, with his energy, tact, initiative, and expertise, he was able to help the German economy. However, in 1915, pressured by the military, the government replaced him with an army general. The argument was simple: the German army command did not like having a Jew in such a sensitive position.

Rathenau's attitude toward his Jewishness was ambivalent. On the one hand, he was proud of his Jewish heritage. But on the other, although he never went so far as converting, he was not an observant Jew by any stretch of the imagination. In fact, some of his ideas were closer to Christian teaching than to those of Judaism, particularly his admiration for the person of Jesus. When he was in his thirties, he met Martin Buber, with whom he discussed the Hasidic movement. The Hasidim appealed to his mystical tendencies, and his acquaintance with their philosophy prompted him to study Hebrew for a time. Like many German Jews, he identified with Germany and admired its blond, Nordic people who, to Rathenau, were exemplified by the Prussian aristocracy. So it is not surprising that when he did his military service, he joined one of the Prussian cavalry guard regiments.

As a Jew who moved in the highest social circles, Rathenau could not but be aware of his ambiguous position in German society. He once said, "In the youth of every German Jew there is a painful moment which he remembers all his life, when he becomes aware for the first time that he is a second class citizen and that all his ability and accomplishment in the world cannot free him from this condition."[3] He regarded Jews as intellectually superior, schooled by centuries of Talmudic learning, but also as "a race governed by fear."[4] Because of the Jews' inferior position in society, he believed, they had a sense of helplessness, and tried to compensate for this by developing their intellects beyond other peoples'. On that subject, he said: "The Jews are the salt of the earth; but you know what happens when one takes too much salt. I have always found that people who are clever and nothing more come to grief even in business. And they richly deserve it; for in themselves they are unproductive."[5] Rathenau addressed himself repeatedly to the Jewish problem, publishing an essay entitled "Hear O Israel" in Maximilian Harden's journal *Zukunft* in 1897, as well as articles on the Jews and the state in *Neue Freie Presse* (from which his above comments on Jews being second class citizens originally came). As he did not feel any kinship to the Orthodox or to the Zionists, Rathenau, like Marx and

Lassalle and many other German Jews, found himself in an equivocal position, never denying his Jewish roots, yet preferring the company of the German aristocrats, but not really at home in either world. At one time, perhaps in an attempt to bridge that gap, he suggested that Jews were no different from other German tribes, no different from Saxons, Swabians, and Wends.

His writings were not limited to Jewish affairs. The stream of books, pamphlets, essays, and articles he turned out covered a great variety of subjects. In fact, he thought of himself as being primarily a thinker and author and believed that his writings were as important as his work in business and finance. On the whole, however, posterity has disagreed with him, although some of his books were best sellers of the day and exerted a considerable influence on the intellectual life of the time. In his 1971 book on Rathenau, David Felix does not rate them very highly: "The books were completely lacking in original ideas, self-indulgent, pretentious in style, and disdainful of proof as they proceeded from one arbitrary statement to the next: the sermons of a masterful moralizer who knows better."[6]

The two works which were the most substantial and aroused the greatest interest were *Mechanism of the Mind* (1913) and *In Days to Come*, which appeared in German in 1917 and was translated into English in 1921. Harry Kessler regards the first as Rathenau's principal work. In his summary of it Kessler says, "He describes *'the birth of the soul'*; and behind his words we seem to see, only thinly disguised, three experiences connected with his

172

visit to Greece: Greek scenery in its sublime grandeur, a new delight in artistic creation, and the urge of a passionate, unfulfilled craving for love."[7] It was not the love between man and woman, however; it was the love of which St. Paul speaks, and his soul was the soul that Spinoza calls the image of God. Although Rathenau never alludes to the sources of his philosophy, it is clear that the ideas in this book were influenced by the New Testament, Hasidic writings, Spinoza, and Johann Fichte.

His second major work, *In Days to Come*, is a very different book, for it deals largely with economic and political questions. Written during World War I, it addresses the future of Germany and the West. Much of it is based upon Marx's ideas, although Rathenau tells us that Marxism was outdated and that he alone was developing a new system that would create a better, more just and rational world. Rathenau hoped to achieve this by doing away with everything extravagant and superfluous. Idleness would be abolished and "all forces would be harnessed to the work of spiritual and material production."[8] At the same time, free competition and private enterprise would be preserved and the responsibility for guiding society would be placed in the hands of those who were most able both intellectually and morally. Inherited wealth would be abolished as far as possible, and there would no longer be any class barriers; gifted children of the proletariat would be able to rise in the world. Most significant of all, perhaps, Rathenau envisaged a powerful state that would control the economy, with planners in charge of production and consumption. Although these ideas aroused a certain interest, some critics pointed out that they were strange ideas for a man of immense wealth who prided himself on his exalted social position. Later critics have noted that, in many ways, his utopia resembles the corporate state advocated by Italian fascists a decade later.

Although Walter Rathenau had been quite influential during the years of the German Empire, his voice listened to with great respect, the fact that he was a Jew precluded his appointment to any high government post. During the war years, he had wielded real power for a brief time as the procurer of raw materials, but his attitude toward the war was skeptical, and he had doubts about Germany's ability to defeat England, which further isolated him. In a statement he made at the time, which his enemies held against him for years to come, he said that "the day will never come when the Kaiser will enter through the Brandenburger Gate as a conquering hero astride a white charger. If that event occurs then the history of the world will have lost all its meaning.

With the establishment of the Weimar Republic and its extension of full rights to Jews, Rathenau's position changed drastically. His well-known and extensive experiences in economic affairs and his many international contacts induced the government to hire him. Rathenau was first asked to help prepare for the 1919 peace conference in Versailles. Then, in 1920, he was made a member of the commission for the socialization of the economy. He also took part in an international conference in Spain in 1920 and he was involved in preparations for the London Imperial Conference of 1921, in which German war damages to the Allies were to be negotiated.

When the leader of the Catholic Center Party, Karl Joseph Wirth—an old friend of Rathenau's—became chancellor in 1921, he named Rathenau minister of reconstruction. The appointment would put him in charge of negotiating the terms for rebuilding the devastated regions of Belgium and northern France at the reparations conferences at Cannes and Genoa. Initially, Rathenau was reluctant to accept, for although he was only fifty-four, he regarded himself as an old man. In a letter written in 1920 to a close friend, he said, "I look backwards rather than forwards and my work is almost done."[9] He also maintained that a Jew should not be too prominent in public life and he was very much aware of his unpopularity in right-wing circles and of the danger such a public position would expose him to. His mother, to whom he was very close, also feared for his safety and strongly urged him to refuse the offer. Nevertheless, after hesitating for days, he decided to accept it, on the grounds that it was his duty as a German to help his country at this crucial time. He hoped that through this ministerial position, he could help advance the cause of peace, for he was convinced that only by cooperating and meeting the demands of the Allies could Germany regain its proper place in the family of nations.

In early 1922, he headed the German delegation to the conference at Cannes. Shortly after his return to Berlin, the German foreign minister abruptly resigned, and Chancellor Wirth once again turned to Rathenau. He did, indeed, seem the most suitable candidate for foreign minister, especially after his intense work at the Cannes conference. Again he hesitated, but in February of 1922 he finally accepted, and with his move, he attained the highest official position that any German Jew has ever held.

As the foreign minister of Germany, Rathenau attended the great international Conference of Genoa, only two months after taking office. In addition to Great Britain, France, Italy, and Germany, the new Soviet Union was also present, their delegation headed by Georgi V. Chicherin who created a stir by advocating universal disarmament. Wirth and Rathenau were anxious to re-establish cordial relations with France and Britain and to reach an agreement on the reparations question. Although Rathenau was ready to negotiate reparation terms with the Allies, the conference quickly became complicated by other issues that revolved around the recent Russian Revolution and the new Soviet government. The Allies had lent money to Russia before and during the war when that country was still under the tsar. Now, the newly formed USSR insisted that it should not be held responsible for those debts and, further, that Germany and the other Allied countries owed it reparations for damages they had inflicted when they had intervened in the Soviet Union after the Russian Revolution.

With the Allies at such cross purposes, no agreement was reached, and the conference adjourned on May 19. Rathenau negotiated and signed the Treaty of Rapallo on Easter Sunday. It is this treaty for which he is most well remembered. Negotiations between the USSR and Britain and France on the issues of trade, cancellation of old tsarist debts, and so forth had reached an impasse. At one A.M., Chicherin called Rathenau to inform him that his delegation was ready to meet Rathenau's in nearby Rapallo, in order to discuss a treaty between the USSR and Germany. Rathenau, who had always advocated a Russian-German rapprochement, was eager to work out a separate agreement with the Soviet Union, and so he went to Rapallo to meet with Chicherin. By the terms of Rathenau's and Chicherin's Treaty of Rapallo, both Germany and the new Soviet Union canceled each other's prewar debts and renounced all war claims. The two countries agreed on trade, as well, with the Soviet Union granting Germany most-favored-nation status; and Germany gave full recognition to the Soviet government.

In summing up Rathenau's accomplishment, Harry Kessler writes:

> Germany, on the other hand, had regained her status as a Great Power. Besides this she was bringing home, in the teeth of the French opposition, her treaty with Russia; and Rathenau had prepared the ground for further advance on the path of negotiation and understanding by establishing relations of mutual confidence with some at

least of the Allied statesmen. After Genoa, Germany was no longer an outcast. In the terrible years which were still in store for her, her new position helped decisively to bring about the collapse of the French ambitions on the Rhine.... It was the intellectual force and steadiness of Rathenau which convinced some of Germany's former enemies that his 'policy of fulfillment' was honest, thus averting these dangers and preparing the way for Germany's slow rise from the abyss.[10]

Rathenau's diplomatic achievements made him one of the most respected statesmen in Europe. But while he was applauded by the democratic forces in Germany, his willingness to arrange for reparation payments under the terms of the earlier Treaty of Versailles aroused implacable hostility among right-wing extremists and anti-Semites. A group of fanatical young nationalists, hating him as a Jew and convinced that he was betraying Germany, decided that he had to be killed. Chancellor Wirth, having been informed of the plot by a priest, warned Rathenau of the danger he faced, but the foreign minister ignored his advice to protect himself with body guards, apparently feeling that if the fates had decided that his time was up, that it had to be. On June 24, 1922, the young assassins shot him as he was being driven from his house in Grunewald to the ministry offices. Although a young nurse tried to help him, and his chauffeur rushed him home, he died shortly afterward.

When the news of Rathenau's assassination spread through the city, hundreds of thousands of mourners gathered under the red banner of the socialists and the black, red, and gold flag of the republic and marched down the main streets of Berlin. The right wing, who had hoped that the assassination of Rathenau would lead to the overthrow of the government, was bitterly disappointed. When their leader appeared in the German parliament where Chancellor Wirth was giving a eulogy, he was greeted with cries of "Murderer! Murderer!" and was forced to leave. Rathenau's funeral took place on June 27. His coffin, draped in a large flag of the republic, lay in state in the Reichstag. President Friedrich Ebert delivered the funeral oration, and great memorial processions were held all over Germany. More than a million people demonstrated in Berlin, a hundred fifty thousand in Munich and Chemnitz, a hundred thousand in Hamburg, Breslau, and Essen. "Never before had a German citizen been so honoured," Kessler said.[11]

Walter Rathenau was mourned not only in Germany but all across Europe. Although Great Britain's David Lloyd George had had his differences with Rathenau, he gave voice to a widespread feeling when he said how much he regretted the death of Dr. Rathenau, which had deprived the German people of one of its most distinguished representatives. "The whole world must honour those who incur the risk of public hatred, as did he, from devotion to their country's good."

NOTES

[1] H.G. Adler, *The Jews in Germany*, (Notre Dame, IN: U. of Notre Dame Press, 1969) 148.

[2] Among the many books on Rathenau, we especially recommend: Count Harry Kessler, *Walter Rathenau: His Life and His Work* (New York: H. Fertig, 1969 [c1928]); David Felix, *Walter Rathenau and the Weimar Republic* (Baltimore: Johns Hopkins Press, 1971); and J. Joll, *Intellectuals in Politics* (New York: Weidenfeld and Nicholson, 1960). See also Walter Rathenau, *Gesammelte Schriften*, (Berlin: S. Fischer, 1925-29), 5 vols.

[3] Quoted in Felix, *Walter Rathenau and the Weimar Republic*, 45.

[4] Quoted in Kessler, *Walter Rathenau: His Life and His Work*, 24.

[5] *Ibid.*, 26.

[6] Felix, 47.

[7] Kessler, 76.

[8] Rathenau, *In Days to Come* (New York: Knopf, 1921), 12.

[9] Quoted in E. Ludwig, *Nine Etched From Life* (New York: McBride, 1934), 163.

[10] Kessler, 357-58.

[11] *Ibid.*, 380.

IX: LITERATURE

In the arts, it is literature for which German Jews are particularly well known. As early as the thirteenth century, the Jewish Minnesänger Süsskind von Trimberg of Bavaria made a notable contribution to medieval poetry, and a representation of the *minnesanger* dressed in the long coat, pointed hat, and heavy beard worn by the Jews of the period appears in the famous Manesse manuscript. But it was not until the nineteenth century that Jewish writers began to emerge as important figures in German letters. Best known in his own time was Berthold Auerbach (1812-1882), whose *Village Tales from the Black Forest* enjoyed great popularity. In the twentieth century, writers of Jewish origin became ever more prominent in all forms of literature. In drama, there was the revolutionary playwright Ernst Toller who for a time enjoyed extreme success; in poetry, Karl Wolfskehl, who belonged to the George circle and ended his life in exile in New Zealand; in history, Rudolf Gundolf, whose books on Goethe and Caesar became classics; in literary criticism, Walter Benjamin, who committed suicide when the Gestapo was about to arrest him; in political satire, Kurt Tucholsky, who killed himself in exile in Sweden; and in biography, the immensely successful Emil Ludwig.

Among the best known German Jewish novelists was Jakob Wassermann (born in Fürth, 1873, died in Altaussee in Austria, 1934). All his early novels are set in his native Franconia. *The Gooseman* (1915) is probably the best of these. It portrays the life of an artist in bourgeois society, showing the difficulties he encounters. His later works, such as *The Maurizius Case* (1928) are absorbing psychological studies which owe a great deal to Dostoevskii. Internationally acclaimed, they made him one of the best known and most popular writers in Germany. In 1921 he also wrote a small volume entitled *My Life as German and Jew*, in which he discussed some of the problems faced by German Jews.

Very different, both as an individual and a writer, was Alfred Döblin (born in Stettin, 1878, died in Freiburg, 1957). He grew up in Berlin where he studied medicine, which he practiced for most of his life. His most famous work was *Berlin Alexanderplatz* (1929). An expressionistic novel about lower-class life in the metropolis, it was very much influenced by Dos Passos and James Joyce. A leftist as well as a Jew, he left Germany

182

after the Nazis took control and went first to France and later to the United States. Unlike most other German Jews, he returned to Germany after the war, but as a cultural officer with the French occupation forces. Unfortunately, Döblin never did regain the literary reputation he had before the war.

A writer whose fate was more typical of the German Jewish experience was Lion Feuchtwanger (born in Munich, 1884, died in Los Angeles, California, 1958). He wrote many successful historical novels, some of which, such as *Sweet Jew* (1925) and his trilogy, *Josephus* (1923), *The Jew of Rome* (1935), and *Josephus and the Emperor* (1942) dealt with Jewish subjects. He, too, was forced to leave his native country and, in 1933, went to France. He was interned in a French concentration camp in 1940, but he managed to escape and get to America, where he spent the rest of his life. In contrast to Döblin, whose work was experimental and innovative, Feuchtwanger was a traditional storyteller whose novels had a large audience both in Germany and the United States.

Another outstanding Jewish novelist of the Weimar period was Arnold Zweig (born in Glogau in Silesia, 1887, died in East Berlin, 1968). Of his many books, by far the best and most internationally acclaimed is his war novel, *The Case of Sergeant Grischa* (1927). Although he wrote many other books after that, none achieved such success. An early Zionist, Zweig emigrated to Palestine in 1933, hoping to find a new home in the land of his ancestors. But with the growing nationalism of the new

HEINRICH HEINE

state, combined with the fact that he was becoming ever more Marxist, he returned to Germany (East Germany) in 1948. Received in East Berlin with great enthusiasm, he became the head of the Academy of Arts of the German Democratic Republic. Although he was one of the most revered literary figures in the former East Germany, he never recaptured the success as a novelist which he had enjoyed during the 1920s.

The most famous of all German Jewish literary figures is no doubt Heinrich Heine. Critics both in his own time as well as today consider him the greatest German poet next to Goethe. A bibliography published some years ago listed no fewer than nine thousand books and articles dealing with Heine, and the number has grown in the intervening years. The first great Heine scholar was Adolf Strodtmann who shortly after the poet's death, issued his complete works in twenty-one volumes and wrote a two volume biography.[1] In both the postwar states of West and East Germany, there was an extensive Heine revival, for his work was banned during the Nazi period. Complete new editions of his writing were issued in Hamburg and Weimar in the 1970s, and the Heine house in Düsseldorf was rebuilt. Today, his popularity continues to grow. No other German poet has enjoyed such widespread renown in the world at large, with translations of his poems appearing in all the European languages, as well as in Hebrew, Japanese, and Arabic.

Heine was born on December 13, 1797, in Düsseldorf

which at the time was not yet part of Prussia, but was the capital of a small Rhenish state that later came under French rule. Both his parents were descended from old Jewish families whose histories went back to the seventeenth century. The child was named Harry after an English business associate of his father, but later in life the poet changed his name to the German Heinrich. His parents were active in the Jewish community and, though they never denied their roots, they were not observant Jews but products of the Enlightenment. They sent their son to a Düsseldorf school run by Catholic priests. Heine often referred to the Bible but always used the Martin Luther translation.

Heine seems to have been quite fond of his parents, although neither of them ever shared nor understood his literary ambitions. His father, apparently a charming if weak man, was in the textile business. His mother was a strong, practical woman who hoped that her son would become a high government official or a rich banker like his uncle Salomon, a self-made millionaire in Hamburg. In 1815, young Heine was sent to Frankfurt to learn the banking business, and two years later went to Hamburg to work in his uncle's firm. He set up his own business in 1818, but it failed miserably, and when it went into bankruptcy in 1819, his career as a businessman came to an end.

Heine's family now decided that he should study law, and his uncle Salomon agreed to pay for his nephew's legal education. At Bonn University, he was particularly attracted by the literature and philosophy lectures of August Wilhelm von Schlegel, one of the chief exponents of the Romantic movement. After two semesters in Bonn, he transferred to Göttingen University, where he got into trouble in connection with a duel, so in 1821, at the age of twenty-three, he returned to Berlin where he studied for the next two years under Hegel. He also frequented the literary salon of Rahel Levin and her husband Varnhagen von Ense as well as that of Elizabeth von Hohenhausen, the German translator of Lord Byron. At the same time, he became a member of the Society for the Culture and Science of Judaism.

Although Heine was never very interested in law, he completed his course of study and received a law degree in 1825. At that time, he aimed at becoming either a professor or a government official, and so he converted to Protestantism, less out of any religious conviction than because he thought that it would help his career. But despite his conversion, which he himself came to regret, he did not succeed in either goal. But writing was beginning to interest him more and more. In fact, the only gainful employment Heine ever had was in 1827, when he worked as an editor of a periodical issued by Goethe's publisher Cotta, but that lasted for only a brief time, and Heine showed little interest in that end of literary work.

Indeed, by this time Heine had emerged as a gifted writer who had published numerous poems in Berlin literary magazines as well as a small volume of verse, two dramas, and several literary essays. The book which

187

established him as an outstanding author was *Die Harzreise* ("Harz Journey," 1826) a combination of realism and irony that was much admired. It was followed by several other travel books that recount the stages of his journey from Munich to the baths of Lucca, in Italy. In the last volume, however, he included personal attacks on the poet August Graf von Platen, pointing out Platen's homosexual tendencies, which aroused a good deal of resentment in literary circles as well as demonstrating for the first time the sharp, bitter side of Heine's wit.

Heine's international fame rests on his *Buch der Lieder* ("Book of Songs," 1827), a collection of poems published when Heine was thirty years old. Many of these poems go back to the period between 1821 and 1824 and often deal with unrequited love. In their simple beauty, they are among the loveliest of lyric poetry in the German language and established Heine as the greatest German poet next to Goethe. They have been set to music by such celebrated composers as Schubert, Schumann, Mendelssohn, and Brahms. Although modern critics have found them too sentimental, their evocation of unhappy love and their settings of moonlight and flowers and singing nightingales have moved generations of readers all over the world. Here, for instance, is a well known example of his work:

Im wunderschönen Monat Mai,	In the beautiful month of May
Als alle Knopen sprangen,	When all the buds were springing,
Da ist in meinem Herzen	There within my heart
Die Liebe aufgegangen.	Love, too, was rising.

188

Im wunderschönen Monat Mai,	In the beautiful month of May
Als alle Vogel sangen,	When all the birds were singing,
Da hab' ich ihr gestanden	I confessed to her
Mein Sehnen und Verlangen.	My desire and longing.[2]

Perhaps the most famous poem in the book is "Lorelei," which tells the story of the beautiful maiden with golden hair whose song lures the passing boatman to his death. This poem had become such a part of the German tradition that when the Nazis tried to suppress Heine's works, they labeled "Lorelei" an anonymous folksong. In addition to the short lyrics, *Book of Songs* also contains ballads that show Heine's debt to German folksongs: "The Grenadier," a ballad about two grenadiers who remain faithful to their hero Napoleon; and "Besazer," which recounts the story of the Babylonian king who, after being warned by mysterious writing on the wall of his palace, is murdered by his own soldiers. Other well-known poems in the collection were written on the island of Norderney and celebrate the beauty and power of the North Sea.

Heine's publisher for these works was Julius Campe of the Hamburg publishing house of Hoffmann and Campe. Although their relationship was sometimes stormy, Heine remained faithful to him and never changed his German publisher. The royalties he received for *Book of Songs* were modest; it sold slowly at first, only becoming an international bestseller later on. But Campe published all of Heine's works, enabling the poet to earn a living from his writing. Modern scholars have calculated that Heine received the equivalent of $370,000 from his publisher during his lifetime.[3]

Heine's other main source of his income was his uncle Salomon. Although he was not over generous and frequently protested that his nephew should get a job like other people and earn his own living, he nevertheless came to his nephew's assistance over and over again. Their sometimes fractious relationship was not helped by the fact that the young Heine fell in love with his uncle's daughters—first, Amalie and later with her younger sister, Theresa. Both affairs were unhappy, but they inspired some of the most beautiful love songs in German literature. Uncle Salomon, probably not without reason, suspected that Heine was pursuing his daughters as much for the wealth they would inherit as for their not inconsiderable charms.

Heine had grown up in Düsseldorf at the time of the French occupation and was an ardent admirer of Napoleon and the French Revolution, and he loved France and French culture. In fact it was this cosmopolitan outlook that many German nationalists have held against him. He celebrated Napoleon—whom most of his contemporaries regarded as a foreign conqueror and tyrant—in *Book of Songs*, *Travel Sketches* (1827-31), and his prose work *The Book of Le Grand* which Sammons called "a genuine masterpiece... the crowning work of his pre-Parisian prose."[4] In this work, Heine gives a somewhat fictionalized account of his childhood, including seeing Napoleon, as well as telling the story of a French drum major named Le Grand. In a later work, he recounts his visit to the battlefield of Marengo, where Napoleon won one of his greatest victories; "Let us praise the French! They are concerned with the two most important needs of human society, good food and civil equality; in the culinary art and in freedom they have made the most progress."[5]

What with his love for France and his own disappointments in Germany, it is not surprising that Heine decided to move to Paris, where he would not only enjoy greater freedom but could win more prestige as a man of letters and have a better chance of making a living. Heine himself said that what persuaded him to move was the July revolution of 1830, but like many other accounts in his autobiographical writing, this is entirely not true, for he did not rush to Paris to join the revolutionaries but made a leisurely trip by way of Frankfurt, Heidelberg, Karlsruhe, and Strassburg. Besides, as he said later, the revolution simply replaced the aristocratic Bourbon royalty with a monied class.

Heine, now thirty-three, arrived in Paris in May of 1831. With the exception of two brief trips to Germany to visit his mother, Paris became his home for the rest of his life; but he never gave up his Prussian citizenship, seeing himself as a German poet living in exile. In fact, the political situation in Germany and the strict censorship in Prussia made it difficult for him to publish and distribute his books there, so whether or not he had originally intended to stay, it seemed quite sensible to remain in the French capital.

Initially he was very happy in Paris and, as he himself

said, he felt like a fish who has entered water. Working as a correspondent for *Augsburger Allgemeine Zeitung*, the most prestigious liberal newspaper in Germany, and contributing to numerous French periodicals, he was not only able to make a living, but he enjoyed more prestige and appreciation in France than he had in his own country. A number of his earlier works, such as his *Travel Sketches*, were now translated into French and he associated with many of the great French writers Balzac, Dumas (père), Sand, Hugo, and Musset—and composers—Berlioz, Liszt, Chopin, and Meyerbeer. Gerard de Nervel became his close personal friend and translator.

Still, Heine never wholly adapted to French society. It is said that he spoke French with a heavy German accent and continued to compose his work in German. Although from 1840 to 1848 the French government paid him a pension intended for distinguished foreign refugees, he never took up French citizenship, which he could have readily attained because he was born in the Rhineland during the period when it was occupied by France. He continued to see himself as a German poet and therefore felt it would be inappropriate to take French citizenship.

Although his poetic output declined in the 1830s, those years were creative ones for Heine as a prose writer. Many of his prose writings originated as articles for German and French newspapers and journals; later, they were edited, supplied with introductions, and published as books in France and Germany. Among them were his accounts of France, entitled *About the French* (published in Hamburg, 1833), in which Heine gives a vivid picture of his impressions of the Parisian scene and the political situation; *History of the Fine Literature in Germany* (published in Germany, 1836); and *The Romantic School* (published in Germany, 1836), an attack on the Romantic movement which Heine called obscurantist, Catholic, and reactionary; and compared unfavorably to the paganism and humanism of Goethe, whom Heine greatly admired. This work, together with his *History of Religion and Philosophy*, was also published in French under the title *D'Allemagne* ("The Germans") in 1835. Between 1834 and 1840, he also brought out a series in four volumes entitled *The Salon*, which deals mostly with the Parisian salons but also contains other pieces including a novel-in-progress, *Der Rabbi von Bacherach*. *Der Rabbi* is his most Jewish work, and it was never finished.

In Heine's private life, the most important event of these years was his marriage to a young woman whom he called Mathilde. The different biographies of Heine suggest that, before meeting his future bride, he had avoided any serious entanglements. However much he had written about love, and how ever great his charm to women, he had never lived with or been close to a woman for any length of time. He was also quite discreet about his love life, so although his romantic style may suggest intimacies, it is most likely that none really occurred. There is no doubt, however, that in Hamburg and even more so in Paris, he consorted with

193

prostitutes, some of whom he even celebrated in his Paris poems.

Mathilde, whose real name was Crescence Eugenie Mirat, was a *giselle*, a working girl, who was employed in her aunt's shop. Heine met he in 1834 when he was thirty-six and she was nineteen. She was an attractive woman of great vitality, but she was uneducated. Some say she was practically illiterate. Certainly, she knew no German, never read his poetry, and—according to Heine himself—did not know that he was a Jew. Her own great fondness for him can be measured by the fact that, after his death, she remained loyal to his memory and never remarried, although several men proposed to her. In the beginning, Heine tried to free himself from his infatuation. But he was unable to. He and Mathilde lived together for some time and, in 1841, were married in a Catholic ceremony in St. Sulpice. Their relationship was often stormy, with Heine constantly complaining about her extravagance, but she seems to have been the kind of wife he wanted and needed. In fact, one is reminded of Goethe who, after many romances with cultured and noble ladies, married his gardener's daughter.

In his own lifetime, Heine was celebrated chiefly as a lyrical poet. Even those who tried to suppress his political writings—as von Metternich of Austria succeeded in doing—greatly admired his *Book of Songs*. But twentieth-century critics, for the most part, regarded his poetry as mere romantic versification and his political polemics and his prose writing as his great achievements. This was especially true in the former East Germany and, since the 1960s among radical students in the former West Germany where Heine has been hailed as a revolutionary, the comrade of Marx and Engels, who had foreseen the rise of a fanatical nationalist movement in Germany and the *furor Germanicus*. It is certainly not pure chance that in the 1960s a ten volume edition of Heine's works and letters, edited by Hans Kaufmann, was published in East Berlin, or that the most complete bibliography of books and articles about Heine was issued, not in his native city of Düsseldorf nor in Hamburg where most of his books were originally published, but in Weimar in the East German Democratic Republic.[6]

Throughout his life, Heine was engaged in political issues. In fact, he said that when he died, a sword should be put on his grave rather than a rose. He fought for intellectual freedom and a more democratic society and was an advocate of greater social justice. If he was disappointed in the July revolution, it was because it did not result in the redistribution of wealth to help the poor. Even before he went to France, his desire for a more just society had attracted him to the ideas of Saint-Simon, the eighteenth century utopian proto-socialist. In Paris, he befriended the leading Saint-Simonist of the day, Barthélmy (Père) Enfantin, to whom he dedicated one of his books. He also met Marx and Engels, with whom he maintained cordial relations. Yet, when the revolution of 1848 occurred, Heine neither favored nor took part in it.

This rather strange contradiction can be accounted for by the fact that his personal feelings and social aspirations were quite different from the political ideas he advocated in his writings. Heine himself admitted that he was an aristocrat by temperament. Although he was not of the traditional nobility, he was certainly one of the intellectual elite. And while he often complained about his poverty and never attained a material wealth comparable to his millionaire uncle or some of the immensely successful French writers like Alexandre Dumas and Victor Hugo, he was never poor in a real sense.

Far from favoring the dictatorship of the proletariat as his radical friends did, he would have preferred a benevolent monarchy in which an enlightened elite ruled over the masses. Heine's misgivings about the masses were most poignantly expressed in the 1855 preface of the French edition of his *Lutetia*.

> Anxiety and terror fill me when I think of the time when these iconoclasts will come to power. Their heavy hands will ruthlessly shatter the marble effigies of beauty so dear to my heart. They will put an end to the whimsical play things of art which the poet cherishes. They will plow up the laurel groves and plant potatoes. They will root out from the soil of society the lilies that neither toil nor spin.... The nightingales, those unnecessary songsters, will be chased away and alas, my *Book of Songs* will serve as bags in which the grocer of the future will wrap coffee and snuff for old women.... Yet this communism, so

threatening to my peace of mind, so opposed to my interests, casts a spell over me.[7]

In addition to the many references to politics and social injustice which are found in his writing, two pieces are always cited as outstanding examples of Heine's socially engaged work, one in *Germany, A Winter Tale*, a long narrative poem of 1843 written after his first trip back to Germany.[8] The other, a much shorter work, is a poem about the plight of the Silesian weavers and was published in his *Late Poems* of 1853-54.[9] As one of his biographers says, "In East Germany, *Deutschland, Ein Wintermärchen* ["Germany, A Winter Tale"] is prized not only as Heine's most important work but as one of the supreme achievements in German literature, out-ranked only by Goethe's *Faust*."[10]

A remark Heine made during his last illness has aroused a great deal of interest, especially among Jewish scholars. He said that he was no longer a follower of Hegel or of a divine being as the Greeks and Goethe were, but "a poor deathly ill Jew."[11] No doubt, the sentiments that the dying Heine expressed demonstrate a heightened awareness of his Jewish roots and may even suggest that he returned to the faith of his fathers.

Heine was never an unmitigated atheist. Where religion was concerned, his animosity was not directed toward the notion of a supreme being. On the contrary, what he disliked was organized religion, whether Christian or Jewish. Like Spinoza before him, he believed for most of his life that God was the absolute infinite, but he did not believe in a Jehovah who intervened in the life of the individual. In his old age, he wrote:

> The stories that are circulating about my present religiosity and piety have been mixed with much nonsense and even more malice. There has not been such a great change in my religious feeling.... I have given up the Hegelian God, or rather the Hegelian godlessness, and in its place I have again pulled out the dogma of a real, personal God who is outside nature and apart from the human mind.... Hegel has sunk very low in my estimation, and old Moses is in the ascendancy. If only I had his prophets along with Moses![12]

These sentiments were expressed in his *Hebräische Melodien*, which formed part of his *Romanzero* poetry volume of 1851.

When one looks at Heine's entire work, especially his prose, he comes across more as a pagan than either a believing Christian or a devout Jew. In his opinion, the two major approaches to life were what he called the Nazarene and the pagan. The first relies on religious dogma and tries to overcome the worldly, sensual aspects of life in the name of some higher spiritual concept, while the other glories in the physical world. From this point of view, there was, according to Heine, little difference between Christianity and Judaism, for both subordinated the flesh to an otherworldly reality. Like Goethe, Heine loved the classical Greek civilization; when he wrote about the gods of the ancients, he spoke of them as if they had really existed in a Golden

198

Age before they were replaced by the religion of the Jews and especially the crucified Jesus of the Christians. In this respect, he anticipated Nietzsche—who greatly admired Heine and saw him as the prophet of a new age.

Much has been written about Heine's last years when the fatally ill poet lay on what he called his mattress grave. As with so many things in his life, the nature of his malady, which had begun to affect him in 1848, when he was fifty, remains mysterious. The traditional opinion was that he had syphilis—and he himself apparently believed that—but according to modern medical opinion, he probably suffered from tuberculosis of the spine. Whatever his affliction was, he spent the last eight years of his life as a completely bedridden invalid. Although he had difficulty reading, he remained in complete control of his mental faculties, and he continued to write both poetry and prose to the day of his death. It should also be said that he showed great courage in coping with his drawn-out, painful, and debilitating disease, a fact which visitors who came to see him always mentioned.

Of all the people who visited him during his illness, the most important in Heine's life was a young woman whom he called Mouche. Sharing the final months of his life with him, she was his last love. A somewhat mysterious figure, she called herself Camille Seldon; modern scholars have established that her real name was Elise Krinitz and that she was born in Prague in 1828. Mathilde, who naturally was not too pleased with this relationship, tolerated it because it meant so much to her husband.

In spite of medical treatment and visits to baths, Heine's condition deteriorated steadily. He died on February 17, 1856, at the age of fifty-eight, and was buried in the Montmartre Cemetery in Paris in a simple ceremony attended by about a hundred people. At his request, the epitaph on his tombstone reads simply, "Here lies a German poet." In later years, a monument was erected at the site of his grave which is still visited by thousands of admirers every year. There is also a monument to Heine in the Bronx, New York, placed there in 1897 to commemorate the hundredth anniversary of his birth. And finally, after World War II, a Heine memorial was erected in his native city of Düsseldorf.

NOTES

[1] Recommended recent books on Heine include Jeffrey Sammons, *Heinrich Heine* (Princeton, NJ: Princeton University Press, 1979); Hanna Spencer, *Heinrich Heine*, (Boston: Twayne, 1982); and Siegbert Salomon Prawer, *Heine's Jewish Comedy: A Study of His Portraits of Jews & Judaism* (Oxford: Clarendon Press, 1983).

[2] Heine, *Book of Songs*.

[3] Sammons, *Heinrich Heine*, 121.

[4] *Ibid.*, 127.

[5] Heine, *Sämliche Schriften*.

[6] Hans Kaufmann, *Heinrich Heine; geistige Entwicklung und Künstlerisches Werk*, (Berlin: Aufbau, 1967).

[7] Quoted in Spencer, *Heinrich Heine*, 47.

[8] Atkins, Heinrich Heine: *Werke* (München: Beck, 1973).

[9] *Ibid..*

[10]Spencer, 80.

[11]Ludwig Marcuse, *Heinrich Heine in Selbstzuengnissen und Bilddokumenten* (Hamburg: Rowohlt, 1960), 152.

[12]Quoted in Spencer, 111-12.

ERICH MENDELSOHN

X: ART AND
   ARCHITECTURE

German Jews who achieved prominence in the visual
arts over the centuries are far fewer than those in
literature. The medieval synagogues generally reflect
the period's dominant Christian architectural style. The
one in Worms, for example, is distinctly Romanesque,
and the one in Bamberg, Gothic. The same illumina-
tions in medieval Bibles, Psalters, and Hebrew manu-
scripts were also executed in the prevailing style of the
period. Some, in fact, may have actually been painted
by Christian artists. Whether or not German Jews avoided
the arts because of the Jewish tradition originating in
Moses' prohibition against the making of graven images
is a question which can be endlessly debated; but the
fact is that German Jews' lasting contributions to the
visual arts are slight in comparison to their contribu-

tions to other fields. In the modern era, Hitler was fond of denouncing modern arts as Jewish and degenerate, but in actuality there were virtually no Jews among the leading German artists of the cosmopolitan Expressionist and Abstract Movements he so despised. While names like Pechstein, Kirchner, and Beckmann may have a Jewish ring to the American ear, none of these well-known German expressionist painters were Jewish.

The first German Jewish painter who achieved a certain prominence was Philipp Veit (born in Berlin, 1793, died in Mainz, 1877), grandson of Moses Mendelssohn. Veit converted to Christianity at the age of twelve, following in the footsteps of his mother, Dorothea, who had converted first to Protestantism and then to Catholicism. After receiving his training as an artist in Dresden and Vienna, he became close to the Nazarene movement, which was dedicated to reviving Christian art. Many of his paintings deal with Christian themes as well as with subjects taken from medieval poetry. The most important period in the development of Veit's style were the years between 1815 and 1830, which he spent in Rome. There, he joined the Brotherhood of St. Luke which had been founded by his friend, J. F. Overbeck, a leading exponent of the Nazarene school of painting. He then moved to Frankfurt where he was appointed head of the Stádel Art Institute, and later, he settled in Mainz where he painted large murals as well as portraits and drawings which were greatly admired by his contemporaries. His best-known painting is probably *The Triumph of Christianity*, done in his Frankfurt years.

Perhaps the most successful German Jewish painter was Daniel Oppenheimer (born in Hanau, 1797, died in Frankfurt, 1882). Immensely popular during his lifetime, he was trained first at the Munich Academy of Art and later in Paris. After spending four years in Rome, he returned to Germany in 1825 and settled in Frankfurt. In contrast to Veit, Oppenheimer's work consists mostly of Jewish subjects, particularly scenes from Jewish family life. It is said that there was no Jewish household which did not have at least a reproduction of one of Oppenheimer's sentimental scenes. He was also known as an accomplished portrait artist who painted well-known Jews, such as Moses Mendelssohn and Heinrich Heine.

The renown of these two painters diminished over time, but the same cannot be said of at least two later German Jewish artists, Max Liebermann and Lesser Ury, whose works have enjoyed a revival in modern Germany. Liebermann (born in Berlin, 1847, died there, 1935) the elder, belonged to an old patrician Jewish family and was related to several prominent German Jews, among them Walter Rathenau. Although he cherished his German roots and refused to convert, he was above all a typical cosmopolitan Berliner, known for his wit and elegant life style as head of the Prussian Academy of Art. An early exponent of Impressionism in Germany, Liebermann was very much influenced by Édouard Manet and the Barbizon school. He was one of the leaders of the 1899 Berlin secessionist movement, which broke away from academic painting and was responsible for introducing French Impressionism to Germany. An enormously gifted painter, he is known for his scenes of working-class life and his portraits, as well as the Dutch landscapes he painted in the 1880s and his Impressionist landscapes of the early twentieth century. In the final years of his life, the Nazi government forbade him to paint. Today, one of his better known paintings, *Ropewalk*, can be seen at the Metropolitan Museum of Art in New York City.

Lesser Ury, (born in Birnbaum, Posen, 1861, died in Berlin, 1931), came from a very different background. In contrast to Liebermann, who never treated Jewish themes in his works, Ury produced religious paintings which expressed the spiritual ardor of the East European Jews with subjects such as Moses, Jeremiah, and the Holy City of Jerusalem. But his best works deal with Berlin, showing the city at night or surrounded by its lakes and forests, all of which he painted in an Impressionist style. Unlike Leibermann, Ury lived in poverty all his life, and his work never gained him success.

A major figure both at home and abroad was the German Jewish architect Erich Mendelsohn.[1] He had his greatest success in the 1920s and, although his influence fell off during the heyday of the international style of modern architecture, more recent years have seen a new appreciation of his work. Today, he is also

206

recognized for his influence on many of the boldest, most imaginative designs in contemporary architecture, such as Eero Saarinen's Dulles Airport and Jorn Utzon's Sidney Opera House. In 1941, the Museum of Modern Art in New York City gave him a retrospective exhibition; the Kunstbibliothek in Berlin staged an exhibition to celebrate the hundredth anniversary of his birth in 1987; and, in 1988, the Cooper-Hewitt Museum in New York hosted a show of his architectural drawings and photographs of his buildings.

Erich Mendelsohn (or Eric as he later spelled his name) was born in Allenstein in eastern Prussia, March 21, 1887. Although his name resembles that of the famous Mendelssohn family of Berlin, there is no connection between them. While most of the descendents of Moses Mendelssohn were converts and belonged to the upper levels of Berlin society, Erich Mendelsohn came from an East European Jewish family of modest means. His father was a merchant and his mother, a musician. From his mother's influence, he had a life-long love of music, always attaching great importance to the fact that he was born on the same day as his favorite composer, Johann Sebastian Bach. His wife, Louise Maas, was a musician, and he played music himself.

At the humanist gymnasium in Allenstein, the young Erich showed great interest in Greek culture, music, and literature, and went on to study architecture at the technical high schools in Berlin and Munich. He received a diploma in architecture in 1912 at the age of twenty-five. From 1912 to 1914, he lived in Munich, designing posters, stage settings, and theater costumes. His first architectural commission was for a crematorium for the Jewish cemetery in his native city, a design which he completed in 1913. While he was in Munich, he became friendly with the members of the *Blaue Reiter* ("Blue Rider") movement, including Franz Marc, Paul Klee, and Wassily Kandinsky. He also became an advocate of Expressionism, an artistic movement which influenced his own style. With these artists, the director Hugo Ball, and the composer Arnold Schönberg, Mendelsohn drew up plans for an Expressionist theater, but the beginning of World War I prevented them from realizing their plans.

Mendelsohn served in the German army during the war years, first on the Russian Front and later in the west. Unlike Alfred Doeblin and Arnold Zweig, for whom the war was a shattering experience, Mendelsohn apparently took it in stride, and used any available time—such as when he was on night watch—to make architectural drawings. These sketches, small in scale and highly imaginative, were his first mature works and already embodied many architectural concepts he would use in later years. Now in the Mendelsohn archive in Berlin, they have often been reproduced in books and were exhibited in the Mendelsohn shows in Berlin and New York.

It is in these sketches that Mendelsohn emerges as one of the great pioneers of modern architecture, anticipating developments which were realized fully only many years later in Le Corbusier's Ronchamp Chapel and Frank Lloyd Wright's Guggenheim Museum, when the proper materials for their construction were widely available. As he said in a letter to his wife: "Steel in combination with concrete, reinforced concrete, is the building material for the new formal expression, for the new style. Its power to sustain tension and compression almost equally will have as a consequence a new logic, its own logic under the laws of statics, its own logic of form, its own harmony, its own natural character."[2]

After the war, Mendelsohn opened an architectural office in Berlin which was to become the center of his professional activity during his years in Germany. In 1919, one of the leading Berlin art galleries, Bruno Cassirer's, exhibited his architectural sketches in a show called "Architekturen in Eisen und Beton." In it were Mendelsohn's drawings for industrial buildings of the future—large warehouses, grain elevators, airplane hangers, railway stations, film studios, automobile factories, crematoria, and exhibition halls. Although Cassirer himself opined that the designs were too visionary, the show was successful. It traveled to Hannover, Hamburg, Breslau, Chemnitz, Stuttgart, and Cologne, and established the thirty-two-year-old architect as the most imaginative and forward-looking in Germany. At this time, too, Mendelsohn received his first major commissions, notably the Steinberg hat factory and the Gustav Herrmann houses in Luckenwalde.

The most important of his early works by far is the Einstein Tower, which he built between 1919 and 1921

209

in Potsdam. This work not only created a sensation, it made him the most famous German architect of the day. Built at the suggestion of Dr. Erwin Freundlich, his friend who worked as Einstein's assistant, the tower was an astronomical observatory which could be used to confirm Einstein's theories. It is a truly Expressionist building in which plastic form and curved ribbon windows are employed effectively, a masterpiece that was widely reproduced in photographs and drawings, especially in architectural magazines, making the name Mendelsohn a household word.

The decade between the Einstein Tower and Hitler's rise to power in 1933 was Mendelsohn's most creative and successful period. Along with Walter Gropius and Mies van der Rohe, he was now one of the leading modern architects in Germany. His Berlin office employed no fewer than forty people, making it the largest architectural bureau in the city. Although his clients were mostly rich Jewish businessmen, he received commissions for a variety of projects from all over Germany as well as from abroad. He was also in constant demand as a speaker and a consultant in architectural matters. As he said at the time, "I am up to my neck in work, and I do not know how to finish it. There are always new and more demanding commissions, constantly requiring greater concentration and greater precision. The most difficult thing is to preserve one's intuition, because only this can raise the level of one's art."[3]

Of all these commissions, the most important were the remodeling of the Mosse publishing house headquarters in Berlin and the design of two department stores for Salomon Schocken in Stuttgart and Chemnitz. The first project, which was carried out between 1921 and 1923, consisted largely of adding to an existing structure, but the Schocken stores, built between 1926 and 1929, were original creations of high order. They show Mendelsohn, now forty and at the height of his career, as the most innovative architect in Germany. He made bold use of modern means of construction, reducing the façades of the buildings to horizontal bands of windows which, especially when they are illuminated at night, create a magic sense of open space, as if the building were not made of solid masonry. These long horizontals are counterbalanced with vertical bands of windows at each end. In the Stuttgart store, the vertical elements of the design consist of a semicylinder and a combination of a curved roof and a column of windows that face the street; in the Chemnitz store, both vertical bands house the staircases. Combining grandeur with simplicity and using steel, concrete, and glass in new and imaginative ways, these structures represent a high point in modern architecture and are still admired as masterpieces of contemporary art.

Another major project of the twenties was the Woga complex on the Kurfürstendamm in Berlin, which occupied Mendelsohn from 1926 to 1928. It was an ambitious attempt to combine a movie theater and a restaurant with residential dwellings. The whole project was not carried out as originally planned, but the Universum movie palace became one of his most outstanding accomplishments. Instead of the customary elaborate Baroque design of movie houses, Mendelsohn created a very simple interior on a long, narrow horseshoe shape whose lines converge on the movie screen's stage. The outside is striking, with rounded forms consisting of bands of windows and a vertical upper structure projecting boldly from the center of the roof. The restaurant and apartment complex are also interesting, given that Mendelsohn never specialized in large-scale housing.

He did build several fine residences for well-to-do clients, however, among them the Sternfeld Villa of 1923 in the western part of Berlin. The most outstanding of these was his own house in Rupenhorn, near Berlin, built between 1929 and 1930. Surrounded by a spacious garden and situated in a beautiful setting overlooking the Havel river, it is in a simple, contemporary style, its most remarkable feature the free-flowing space of its interior. Many houses of similar design have been built by others since then, but at that time, it was a striking departure from tradition.

Mendelsohn's last major building before he left Berlin was the Columbushaus at the Potsdamer Platz, completed in 1931 and 1932. Like many of his important works, it has not survived, which is a pity because it was considered one of the most beautiful office buildings ever built. A tall edifice with a strong vertical thrust, its horizontal windows, separated by bands of cement, were layered one over the other, creating a sense of dynamic power. The façade was curved, thus counterbalancing what might otherwise have been a somewhat rigid design, and the two upper floors were separated from the main structure, adding an interesting variation to the design. Ironically, the Columbushaus, Mendelsohn's last German masterwork, ended up as the headquarters for the Gestapo in Nazi Germany.

Well before his forced emigration in 1933, Mendelsohn had had clients outside of Germany. As early as the 1920s, he was invited to lecture in Amsterdam, Den Hagg, and Rotterdam. He met members of Holland's De Stijl group, most notably the architects Pieter Oud and Marinus Dudak. In 1923, the Palestine government asked him to design a new power station, but like many of his projects, such as his plans for a commercial center in Haifa or a garden city on Mt. Carmel, this was never realized. He and the American architect Richard Neutra, however, won the first prize in the competition for the design of the Haifa commercial center.

What was much more important for his career was his visit to the United States, which was financed by the Mosse publishing company. There, he met Frank Lloyd Wright, the architect he most admired and whom he visited at Taliesin East, Wright's home in Spring Green, Wisconsin. In 1925 to 1926, he made a number of trips to the Soviet Union as a consulting architect for the design of a large textile factory at Krasniye Snamya near Leningrad—the Soviets had admired his Steinberg hat factory in Luckenwalde. One of the fruits of these various trips were two books, published in 1926 and 1929. The first was called *Erich Mendelsohn, Amerika,*

213

Bilderbuch eines Architektes and the second, *Erich Mendelsohn, Russland, Europa, Amerika, ein Architektonischer Querschnitt.* Both were illustrated with photographs by the author and published by Mosse, whose headquarters he had designed.

By 1932, when he was forty-five years old, Mendelsohn had achieved everything an architect could desire: world fame, more commissions than he could handle, and the dream house he had built for himself and his wife on the outskirts of Berlin. Besides all this, he had been invited to lecture in England in 1930, where he had been made an honorary member of the Arts Club of London, and he had been elected to the Prussian Academy of Arts, the most prestigious society of its kind in Germany. In 1931, he had been asked—along with Poelzig, Gropius, and Le Corbusier—to enter the competition for a design of the Palace of the Soviets in Moscow. He had also gone to Paris in connection with the founding of the Academie Européenne Mediterranée, and he had been asked to give a lecture in Zurich for the International Society for Cultural Cooperation.

The advent of Hitler in 1933 brought all this to an abrupt end. The first sign came when Mendelsohn was not included among the thirty leading German architects who were asked to submit their designs for a new building for the Reichsbank in Berlin. But unlike the many German Jews who clung to their belief in their beloved *Vaterland*, Mendelsohn—who had been a Zionist for many years and held left-wing sympathies—read the signs correctly, and in March of 1933 moved to England, leaving everything he owned behind.

Mendelsohn's attitude toward his Jewish heritage was never ambiguous. Unlike Marx and Heine, who married gentiles, or Buber, whose wife was a Catholic who converted to Judaism, Mendelsohn married a Jewish woman. While he did not observe the religion of his ancestors, he always considered himself a Jew rather than a German. In a letter to his wife, written in 1923, he called himself an "East Prussian Oriental."[4] No doubt this sentiment had something to do with the fact that he descended from Jews who came from a part of Germany which today belongs to Poland.

The position that Mendelsohn took on the Jews in 1933 was not one which most German Jews of the time could have endorsed:

> The Jews are the only people on earth without a native soil or a national unity—a people which seeks the hospitality of all the world. As this hospitality has been granted for thousands of years, for centuries in Germany, whole districts have been influenced by Jews through the mingling of blood and ideas. All efforts to become one with the native people—compulsory through the inquisition, voluntary through assimilation—have failed. As by a miracle the Jews are the only people of ancient times to retain their individuality: blood, language, mentality, and religion, in spite of continual wanderings without a country, in spite of their subjection to physical and moral influences, persecution and bitter tribulation the world over—down the centuries.[5]

215

In London, Mendelsohn went into partnership with the Russian-born English architect Serge Chermayev, but his only major commission in England was the design for the De La Warr Pavilion in Bexhill, Sussex, which was built between 1934 and 1935. A beautiful structure distinguished by its great, projecting, semicircular balconies, it was a landmark in the development of modern architecture in England. Two other large projects—one, a hotel with a multistory car park for the city of Blackpool—were never executed. In fact, the only Mendelsohn structures besides the De La Warr Pavilion that were actually built were two private houses. As early as December 1934, he had written that England was an "interregnum,"[6] and, in 1935, he set up an architectural office in Jerusalem. When Britain went to war in 1939, he moved to Palestine.

Mendelsohn's new career began with major projects for Hebrew University and for a Hebrew medical center on Mt. Scopus in Jerusalem, as well as for the Chaim Weizman and Salomon Schocken houses. In these buildings, he tried to adopt the design to the Moslem architecture of the surrounding countryside. The result was more solid, less open, structures in which the primary material was stone, with glass and steel less prominent. Describing his new situation in a letter written in Jerusalem in 1935, he wrote: "I am here as an English architect, and I am reminded of our tears-and-Bach country only in bad dreams and in flashes of boundless ignominy. We—Louise and I—are just about to rent an old Arab windmill for an office and home. We see the future as

full of changes and only desire *Cathargo esse delendam.*"[7]
However, he was never to accomplish all he wished to,
mostly because all building activity was stopped in the
British mandate; and so, in 1941, Mendelsohn decided
to move to America.

Although he never lost his enthusiasm for new projects,
the years in the United States must have been quite
disappointing for Mendelsohn. Arriving in New York
after a roundabout trip which took him to Basra, Karachi,
Bombay, and Capetown, he first traveled around the
country, meeting with Albert Kahn in Detroit, Frank
Lloyd Wright at Taliesin East, and Mies van der Rohe
in Chicago. Although he was famous and his 1941
retrospective exhibition at the Museum of Modern Art
traveled to Chicago and San Francisco, Mendelsohn did
not receive any important commissions. And after the
United States entered the war, all major building activity also ended in America. As a result, Mendelsohn
spent the war years studying, writing, and giving occa-
sional lectures, notably the ones at the University of
California at Berkeley which were later published in
book form.

At the end of the war, Mendelsohn moved to San
Francisco, his favorite American city, where he once
more opened up his own architectural firm. In 1947, he
was appointed professor of architecture at Berkeley and
as a practising architect again, embarked upon the last
phase of his distinguished career.

Of his San Francisco projects, the most important was

the design for Maimonides Hospital, completed in 1950. He also designed a San Francisco house for Leon B. Russel. But his most significant American buildings were the synagogues and community centers he designed in St. Louis; Cleveland; Grand Rapids, Michigan; and Minneapolis. The last was not completed until after his death in 1954. Their most distinctive feature is the flexible inner space which can be enlarged for special occasions such as the High Holy Days. However, it has been remarked that none of these works have the boldness or the originality of the best of his German designs. Although he never regained the extraordinary success he had achieved during the 1920s in his native land, he had a long and fruitful career. His death not only prevented him from enjoying the renewed interest in his work that came about in recent years, it deprived the world of one of its most distinguished architects.

NOTES

[1] For further reading on Mendelsohn and his work, we recommend: Bruno Zevi, *Erich Mendelsohn* (New York: Rizzoli, 1985); Arnold Whittick, *Erich Mendelsohn* (London: L. Hill, 1956); Hans Rudolf Morgenthaler, *The Early Sketches of Architect Erich Mendelsohn (1887-1953)* (Lewiston, NY: E. Mellem Press, 1992); Erich Mendelsohn, *Letters of an Architect*, Intr. by Sir Nikolaus Pevsner (London & New York: Abelard Schuman, 1967); and, Erich Mendelsohn, *Works* (New York: Princeton Architectural Press, c1992).

[2] Mendelsohn, *Letters of an Architect*, 32.

[3] Quoted in Zevi, *Erich Mendelsohn*, 100.

218

[4] Mendelsohn, 60.

[5] Whittick, *Eric Mendelsohn*, 199.

[6] Zevi, 141.

[7] Mendelsohn, 142.

Felix Mendelssohn-Bartholdy

XI: MUSIC

In German cultural life, a number of Jews gained preeminence in music. Many of the most celebrated German performers and conductors came from Jewish families, as did a number of well-known musicologists and music critics. German Jews were also important patrons of music and formed a large part of the German music-loving public. (We should note here that two of the world's most famous Jewish composers, Gustav Mahler and Arnold Schoenberg, being Austrian Jews, fall outside our discussion.)

The first important German Jewish composer was Giacomo Meyerbeer, whose real name was Jacob Liebmann Beer. Born in 1791 in Berlin to a prominent German Jewish family, he died in Paris in 1864. A student of Karl Friedrich Zelter, the friend of Goethe, and Georg Joseph Vogler, Meyerbeer was one of Germany's greatest operatic composers. In 1816, he went to Italy where, inspired by Rossini, he composed a number of operas in the Italian manner. He moved to Paris in 1826 and attained his greatest success there. Working in the style of the French grand opera, he produced some splendid works, notably *Robert Le Diable* (1831), *Les Huguenots*, considered his masterpiece (1836), and *L'Africaine* which was produced in 1865, a year after his death. In 1842, King Frederick William IV of Prussia appointed him general director of the Berlin Opera, a signal honor for a German Jew.

Another well-known Jewish composer was Jacques (Jacob) Offenbach (born in Cologne, 1819, died in Paris, 1880). His father, Isaac Juda Eberst, was a cantor in a synagogue and came from Offenbach. Isaac felt that opportunities for Jews in Germany were too limited, so he sent his fourteen-year-old son to France, which he saw as the land of liberty and equality. It was in Paris that Jacob changed his name to Jacques. He spent the rest of his life in France and, indeed, is often referred to as a French composer, not German. He studied at the Paris conservatory and, from 1855 to 1866, wrote music for the opera-comique as well as for theaters and varieté shows. The years of France's Second Republic were his most successful. He gained immense popularity for his lively, satiric operettas, of which he composed more than a hundred, among them *La Belle Helene* (1864) and *La Vie pariesienne* (1866). But he is best remembered for his one serious work, the opera *Tales of Hoffmann*, which was not staged until a year after his death. Offenbach's popularity began to decline after the birth of the Third Republic in 1870. He made various attempts to revive his reputation, but not even a tour of the United States in 1876 regained him the success he had previously known. However, the twentieth century has seen major revivals of his work, including the making of a filmed version of *Tales of Hoffmann* in the 1950s.

Of the many well-known German Jewish conductors, probably the most famous is Bruno Walter (born in Berlin, 1876, died in California, 1962). He was born Bruno Walter Schlesinger, which suggests that his family—like that of many prominent German Jews—had originally come from Silesia. Walter completed his studies at the Stern Conservatory in Berlin, then began what would become a brilliant career as a conductor, first in Cologne and then Hamburg. In 1901, he became the conductor of the Vienna State Opera, a position to which he was appointed by Gustav Mahler. In 1912, he moved to Munich, where he was musical director of the Munich Opera. He returned to his native city in 1925 as the conductor of the Berlin Municipal Opera. During this period, he also made numerous appearances as a guest conductor across Europe and in the United States. He ended the European phase of his career as conductor of the Gewandhaus concerts in Leipzig. When the Nazis came to power, Walter emigrated to the United States where he became the conductor of the New York Philharmonic, as well as a guest conductor of the Metropolitan Opera, the NBC Symphony, and several other musical ensembles. He was also something of a composer and author. His biography of Gustav Mahler and his own autobiography are still widely read today.

Of the twentieth-century German Jewish composers, the most popular was Kurt Weill (born in Dessau, 1900, died in New York, 1950). A student of Wagner's friend Engelbert Humperdinck and Bussoni in Berlin, he developed a highly original style influenced by both jazz and modern music, which is most evident in such masterworks as his *Three Penny Opera* (1928) and *The Rise and the Fall of the City of Mahagonny* (1930). With Berthold Brecht as librettist and with his wife Lotte Lenya in the leading roles, these works not only created a sensation in Germany but went on to win wide acclaim abroad. Bitterly attacked by the Nazis even before Hitler came to power, Weill fled the country in 1933, going first to Paris and then to New York. In America, he began writing musicals, usually with Maxwell Anderson. Among them were *Lady in the Dark* (1941) and *One Touch of Venus* (1943 with book by Ogden Nash). He also wrote some instrumental music and cantatas, most notably the 1929 cantata *Lindbergh's Flight*. His work enjoyed enormously successful revivals in America in the 1960s and 1970s.

The German Jewish composer to reach the topmost ranks was Felix Mendelssohn-Bartholdy. But his reputation has fluctuated over the years:

The idol of the Victorian parlor, adored by the German and English bourgeoisie alike, the ever-virtuous, angelic, sentimental Mendelssohn of our grandparents' day is a popular fiction. [Then there is] the inveterate, ultra conservative enemy of all *Zukunftsmusik* (in the sense of Wagner's cohorts) … and the effeminate pietist and weakling, as depicted by that nondiscriminating critic G.B. Shaw—these and other similar portrayals of Mendelssohn vanish, like so many webs of fantasy, when confronted with the totality of the original sources.[1]

The truth lies somewhere in between, for while Mendelssohn may have been overestimated by his contemporaries and underrated by the following generation in its rejection of Victorian sentimentality, today he is regarded as one of the major German composers of the nineteenth century, and his works form part of the standard repertory of orchestras throughout the world.

Jacob Ludwig Felix Mendelssohn was born in Hamburg on February 3, 1809, the eldest son of Abraham Mendelssohn who in turn was the son of the great philosopher Moses Mendelssohn. Although Abraham is said to have complained that he started out as the son of a famous father and then became the father of a famous son, he was actually a remarkable person in his own right. A successful banker as well as a man of culture and learning, he married the daughter of one of Berlin's richest and most prominent Jewish families, Lea Itzig, a young woman who knew French and English, could recite Homer in Greek, and was an accomplished musician trained in the tradition of Johann Sebastian Bach. She and her husband had a salon in Berlin which was frequented not just by the elite of Jewish society, but also by prominent non-Jews, among them Napoleon's ambassador to the Prussian court.

Felix, an extremely gifted and sensitive child, was tutored at home. He received an excellent humanistic education and, even more important in light of his later career, his mother taught him to play the piano. When he was seven years old, his father took him to Paris where he studied with the well-known music teacher Marie Bigot; but his most influential teacher was Karl Friedrich Zelter, the head of the Berlin Singakademie. Zelter, an excellent teacher, immediately recognized the extraordinary gifts of his pupil and, in 1818 when the boy was only nine years old, he let him play in a chamber concert. In the following year Felix entered Zelter's academy, an astonishing feat for a mere child. He composed his first works at the age of eleven. When he was twelve, Zelter took his pupil to meet the aged Goethe in Weimar, a visit which made a lasting impression on the boy.

It was at this time that his parents and he and his sister Fanny, to whom he was very close, converted to protestant Christianity. There can be little doubt that the elder Mendelssohns took this step not from any deep religious conviction, but because they believed it would open doors for their children which might otherwise have remained closed. And it seems that the young Felix had already met with some anti-Jewish rebuffs and insults which had greatly upset him. Both his parents were children of the Enlightenment, both had believed in humanistic and moral values above any particular religious faith. Nevertheless, whatever *their* motivations may have been, Mendelssohn took Christianity seriously and wrote several compositions of a definitely religious character.

When Mendelssohn's parents converted a few years later, Abraham and Lea decided that this branch of the family should also change its name. They chose the name Bartholdy. It was the name that Felix's uncle, an art expert and a scholar, had taken when he had converted. (It was actually the name of a large garden which the uncle had acquired in Berlin.) But the young composer refused to go along with his father, choosing instead to call himself Felix Mendelssohn-Bartholdy, a name he kept all his life and which is still used by his descendents today.

Although his parents fully appreciated their son's great musical gifts, they questioned whether it would be possible for him to make an adequate living as a musician. In order to resolve this question, his father took him to Paris in the spring of 1825 to meet Luigi Cherubini, one of the most revered and influential Italian composers of the day. The result was a great victory for Felix because Cherubini, then in his 60s, realized that the sixteen-year-old was a musical genius and enthusiastically encouraged his desire to pursue a musical career.

On his return to Berlin, Mendelssohn began to produce a string of compositions, including a symphony, an opera, piano and string quartets, and an octet for strings. In 1826 at the age of seventeen, he had his first great triumph with his Overture to *A Midsummer Night's Dream*. It was an immediate success and has remained one of Mendelssohn's most popular pieces to this day. Celebrating the genius of Shakespeare who at that time was greatly admired in Germany, the Overture embodied the very essence of romantic sensibility. Indeed, it made Mendelssohn famous, establishing him as one of the greatest German composers of the period. His position in the musical world of Berlin was further enhanced when, against great odds, he conducted J.S. Bach's *St. Matthew Passion* in 1829, a work which had not been performed since Bach's death 79 years before. The event had far-reaching repercussions, re-establishing Bach's position as one of Germany's greatest composers and bringing added renown to Mendelssohn as a conductor.

At this point, Felix Mendelssohn-Bartholdy was only twenty years old, but he was a leading figure in Berlin's cultural life and a young man of great charm and exquisite manners. It was now a logical step for a young musician of his position to go abroad, so not long after he had conducted Bach, he traveled to England. He had two close musical friends in London and letters of introduction to influential members of British society. His visit there proved a triumph and he remembered it with fondness and gratitude for the rest of his life. He was received warmly by great noblemen like the Duke of Devonshire and the Marquis of Landsdown, and he met the opera divas Maria Malibran and Henriette Sontag and the most prominent English composers of the day. As a convinced liberal, Mendelssohn was also impressed by his visit to Parliament. He often spoke of his admiration for the city of London, so much larger and more cosmopolitan than Berlin. In his travels through Scotland, he was similarly taken by the city of Edinburgh.

The climax of Mendelssohn's visit came when the London Symphony Orchestra performed his C-Minor Symphony to great acclaim. The leading musical periodical in London, *Harmonium*, commented on the work: "It is not venturing too far to assert, that his latest labour, the symphony of which we now speak, shews a genius for great writing; and it is a fair presumption, that, if he perseveres in his pursuit, he will in a few years be considered as the fourth of that line which has done such immortal honour to the most musical nation in Europe."[2] As the program that evening had included works by Mozart, Weber, Händel, Rossini, and Cherubini, this was the height of praise for a composer so young. On the same occasion, he was made an honorary member of the Philharmonic Society and asked to conduct his Overture to *A Midsummer Night's Dream*.

In 1880, Mendelssohn traveled to Munich and Vienna, and was well-received in both cities. Next he went to Italy, where he visited Bologna, Florence, and, at last, Rome. Here, too, he was the center of attention and met many prominent composers and musicians, among them Berlioz (whom he enjoyed as a person although he intensely disliked his music). However, his experiences in Italy, especially with Italian opera, convinced him that he belonged to the Northern rather than the Italian school. After his return to Germany, via Switzerland—which would become one of his favorite countries—he took off on another trip, this time to Paris. In the French capital, he made the acquaintance of Liszt and Chopin, the rising stars of the Parisian musical world.

Mendelssohn was not just sightseeing during this time; he was also composing. Some of his works of this period are among his most remarkable achievements: the first version of *Hebrides* Overture; *First Walpurgisnight*, based on Goethe's ballad on the same theme; the immensely popular *Songs Without Words*; various religious choral works; and Piano Concerto in G-Minor, which had its premiere in Munich in October 1831. It was at this time that he began working on the *Scottish* and *Italian* Symphonies, which are among his most enduring compositions. Another work written at this period was his *Reformation* Symphony. Although *Reformation* had little success and he himself was not entirely satisfied with it, today it is considered one of Mendelssohn's most original compositions. It and the chorals and hymns he wrote in Rome give expression to his protestant faith in reaction to the Catholic atmosphere of the Eternal City.

The great centers of European culture were stimulating to the young composer, but notwithstanding the cordial receptions he received, he decided to return to Germany and make his contribution to the musical life of his native country. His old mentor Zelter had died while he was away, and the directorship of the Berlin Singakademie was now open. At the urging of his family and friends but against his own better judgement, Mendelssohn applied for the position. Although his father and great aunt had been generous patrons of the Singakademie, Mendelssohn lost the election to the seat, a blow from which he never fully recovered. Just why he was rejected is not clear, but modern scholars tend to think that anti-Semitism was definitely a factor.

Despite this setback, his career continued to flourish. The London Symphony invited him to write a symphony for them, and he was asked to become the music director of the Lower Rhine Festival in Düsseldorf, which to a certain extent compensated for his rejection in Berlin. The directorship in Düsseldorf was a position of great responsibility but did not suit his temperament; as he himself said, it entailed endless arguments about money and administrative detail. Although his concerts were well received and gave him the opportunity to conduct some of his favorite works, he resigned on very short notice in 1834. The following year, he accepted an appointment as the conductor of the Gewandhaus concerts in Leipzig, a city with which he remained connected for the rest of his life.

Mendelssohn's work with the Gewandhaus concerts was a success, for he greatly improved both the programs and the orchestra. He conducted the works of his favorite composers—Bach, Händel, Mozart, Beethoven, Weber, and Schubert—and the audiences loved the concerts. He traveled to other cities as guest conductor and, in 1836, served once again as the musical director of the Lower Rhine Festival, where he conducted the first performance of his *St. Paul* Oratorio, a work which was much admired during his lifetime. In Frankfurt, he conducted the St. Cecilia Choir and, in 1837, visited London again and then conducted the Birmingham Festival, where the performance of *St. Paul* Oratorio won high praise.

These years were a crucial period in Mendelssohn's personal life. He met Robert Schumann, who became a dear friend and admirer, and Richard Wagner, who became his enemy and most persistent critic. The happiest event of this time was his marriage to Cecile Jeanrenaud, whom he had met in Frankfurt where she had been in the choir. She came from a Swiss-German-Huguenot family, which had settled in Frankfurt where it had become part of the patriciate. Felix, who was taken by her grace and beauty, fell in love with her at their first meeting. Unlike the many sophisticated women he had encountered, she apparently had little interest in music; but their marriage was happy, and she was devoted to her husband and their four children. The saddest event of these years was the death of his father, to whom he had been extremely close and who had played such an important role in his life.

How famous Mendelssohn was in his lifetime is indicated by the fact that when he was in England on a concert tour in 1842, Queen Victoria and Prince Albert invited him to Buckingham Palace where the prince played Mendelssohn's music and the queen sang some of his songs. As well, the king of Prussia, who hoped to turn Berlin into a great cultural center, did everything in his power to persuade the composer to return to his native city. Although Mendelssohn was reluctant to return to Berlin, he agreed in 1841 after long negotiations to become director of the music section of the newly established Academy of Arts, as well as the royal composer for Frederick William IV and the supervisor of protestant church music at the Berlin Cathedral. But he continued to conduct and teach in Leipzig, to direct music festivals in Düsseldorf, and to make triumphant concert tours in England. It was also during this time (1842-43) that he helped to found the Leipzig Conservatory. Because his health was never robust, some of his biographers have suggested that all this hectic activity may have contributed to his early death.

The Berlin experience turned out to be a disappointment, despite the generous terms that had been granted to the composer. The Prussian bureaucracy was difficult to deal with and the Academy of Arts resisted his attempts to develop it. At the king's request, Mendelssohn conducted a series of symphonic and choral concerts in Berlin and wrote various new pieces, notably some music for Sophocles' *Antigone*, Racine's *Athalie*, and Shakespeare's *Midsummer Night's Dream*. He also performed at the Sunday musicales at his sister Fanny's house, which were attended by the elite of Berlin society.

The year of Mendelssohn's thirty-fifth birthday, 1844, was a most productive one. Severing his connections with Berlin, he settled in Frankfurt, his wife's native city, in order to devote himself to his composing and his family. The most famous composition of this year was his Violin Concerto in E-Minor, which he finished in Soden, near Frankfurt, on September 16, 1844. The last of his larger orchestral works, it won great applause at the time and has been highly regarded ever since. Some modern critics have reacted unfavorably to it, but the well-known music critic Philip Radcliffe says of the concerto: "In this work Mendelssohn crystalized with complete success his experiments in the handling of the concerto form, and it stands on the same high plane as the 'Italian' Symphony as a comparatively light but highly polished masterpiece, of the kind for which there is always room."[3]

A work quite different in spirit, and much more ambitious, was Mendelssohn's Oratorio *Elijah*, his major composition of 1845-46, which was finished late in July and had its premiere at the Birmingham Festival in August. Based on an Old Testament text and written in the tradition of the great Händel and Bach oratorios, it was well received at the festival and has been called by some the greatest oratorio of the nineteenth century. It is curious that while Mendelssohn used a text provided by a Christian theologian and presented the material in accordance with traditional Christian church music, he announced the appearance of Jesus Christ with a Jewish theme from a song that had been played on the High Holy Days in the synagogues of his youth. Werner points this out in his book on Mendelssohn and suggests that the composer may have done this quite unconsciously; but it is interesting that Mendelssohn's Jewish heritage does manifest itself when he deals with an Old Testament subject.

In spite of poor health, Mendelssohn continued his feverish activity even into what would be the last year of his life. With all his successes, he still had one unfulfilled dream—to write an opera. When he met and befriended the famous coloratura soprano Jenny Lind (the "Swedish nightingale"), he was inspired anew and began working on one with his customary diligence. Of the several subjects he considered, the one he carried furthest was called *Lorelei* with a libretto by the well-known German poet Emanuel von Geibel. He was also writing *Christus*, an oratorio, but only a small section of this was completed.

In the spring of 1847 he made his tenth and last concert tour in England. It was a great success, but the strain of it further undermined his health. Soon after his return, his sister Fanny died at age forty-two. Felix was grief-stricken and saw this as an omen of his own death, a foreboding which turned out to be true, for he died on November 4, 1847, in his thirty-ninth year.

Mendelssohn's early death came as a great shock to musicians and music lovers throughout the world. In

Germany and throughout Europe and in the United States as well, tributes were paid to the great composer. Untold numbers of concerts of his music were performed in his memory, most notably in Leipzig, London, Vienna, Berlin, Frankfurt, and Paris. For the first week after his death, the Gewandhaus concerts devoted most of their programs to his music. In London, the Sacred Music Society performed his *Elijah*, with the orchestra dressed in mourning. A year after his death, Jenny Lind, who frequently had sung his music in England, organized a memorial service. Its proceeds were used to establish a Mendelssohn foundation for giving scholarships to promising young English and Irish composers. A monument (destroyed by the Nazis in 1937) was erected at the Gewandhaus in Leipzig, and an International Mendelssohn Society, now centered in Basel, was established.

[1] Eric Werner, *Mendelssohn: A New Image of the Composer and His Age*, (Westport, CT: Greenwood Press, 1978, c1963), 10. How greatly Mendelssohn was admired throughout the Victorian era is evident in the numbers of books written about him in that period. Some excellent ones include Wilhelm Adolf Lampadius, *Felix Mendelssohn-Bartholdy: Ein Denkmal für seine Freunde* (1849); Benedict, *A Sketch of the Life and Works of the Late Felix Mendelssohn-Bartholdy* (1850); H. Barbedette, *Felix Mendelssohn: sa vie et ses oeuvres* (1869); Sebastian Hensel, *Die Familie Mendelssohn* (1879). Among recent works worth consulting are: *Felix Mendelssohn, A Life in Letters* (New York: Fromm International Pub. Corp., c1986); and Mozelle Moshansky, *Mendelssohn, His Life and Times* (Neptune, NJ: Paganiniana Publications, c1981).

[2] Quoted in *Ibid.*, 147.

[3] Philip Radcliffe, *Mendelssohn* (London & New York: Farrar, Straus, Giroux, 1967), 111.

XII: WOMEN

Until the nineteenth century, there were very few women outside of royal families who made their mark on the world anywhere, whether Jewish or non-Jewish. The view of German Jews, that "a woman's place is in the home," was not unlike that of the rest of German society; indeed, it was probably adhered to more ardently. Still, like their non-Jewish counterparts, many Jewish women managed their family estates and helped in family businesses, in some cases actually running the family enterprise discreetly from behind the scenes.

It was not until the twentieth century, when these limiting attitudes toward women began to change, that German Jewish women began to make their mark on the cultural and intellectual life of Germany, most especially in politics, philosophy, and literature.

But even before the nineteenth century, there were a few German Jewish women who managed to surmount the social obstacles and attain a degree of success in their own rights. Among these was the author Glückchen von Hameln, better known today as Glückel (born in Hamburg, 1646, died in Metz, Alsace, 1724). Her autobiography is considered a classic and is still widely read today.[1]

Glückel composed the work in Yiddish in 1690 and addressed herself to her children and grandchildren. Living in a self-contained Jewish community which made contact with the non-Jewish world only at the margins, she paints a vivid picture of the life of a wife, mother, and businesswoman in seventeenth-century Germany. Her book is filled with a wealth of personal events: births and deaths, joys and sorrows, business gains and loses, weddings and burials. Glückel von Hameln started out as a petty trader who sold ribbons, hardware, and cutlery from door to door. She later attended trade fairs and dealt in gold and jewelry, and she ended up as a well-to-do merchant who lent money and discounted bills of exchange. Hers was a successful life outside the home, and yet how precarious the position of Jews was in Germany is illustrated by her description of persecutions, including the expulsion of Jews from her native city. What sustained her throughout her life was her religious faith. It not only guided her, it also gave her the certainty that a just God watched over her and her family.

★ ★ ★

Nineteenth-century European society is remembered for the literary salons that blossomed in the capitals. Some of the most famous and beloved hostesses of these salons were German Jewish women:

> By the opening of the nineteenth century,... Jewish salons in Berlin were well established as the center of German social life. The Jews, after all, were charming and witty hosts and hostesses; they were untrammeled by feudal traditions; they were plastic in their adaptability, alert to new literary and artistic developments. Writers, artists, intellectuals, and *viveurs* all found good food and even better conversation at these gatherings; while the clever and vivacious Jewish women who presided as hostesses delighted and fascinated their guests.[2]

The most famous of these women was Rahel Antoine Levin (1771-1883), an extremely intelligent and charming woman who, at the age of forty, married a twenty-six-year-old Prussian diplomat, Karl August Varnhagen von Ense. His extensive writings give a vivid account of his brilliant wife and her salon, which for a time was the vital center of Berlin's intellectual and literary world. Her gatherings were frequented by the leading spirits of the Romantic movement—Achim von Arnim, Clemens von Brentano, Heinrich von Kleist, Heinrich Heine, Karl Maria von Weber, and Goethe, her most venerated guest. Mingling with these literary lights were members of the Prussian nobility and the European intelligentsia; such distinguished figures as the naturalist and world-traveler Alexander von Humboldt and the political leader Ferdinand Lassalle could often be found at Rahel's exchanging ideas and engaging in cordial, cultivated discussion.

Another Jewish-born hostess of the Berlin salons of this period was Henriette Herz. Born in Hamburg, she came from a Portuguese Jewish family named De Lenos. At the age of fifteen, she married Markus Herz, a physician and philosopher who was more than twice her age. They were highly cultured people and held a stimulating salon where she presided and he gave lectures on Kant and other topics. Henriette was famous for her intellect as well as her beauty; she was fluent in Greek, Latin, Hebrew, French, Spanish, Italian, Portuguese, and English. Many of the outstanding figures of the day were her friends, among them Goethe, Schiller, Alexander von Humboldt and his brother Wilhelm, the statesman and school-reformer; the famous novelist Jean Paul Richter, the great historian Barthold Niebuhr; and the leading Kantian philosophers Friedrich von Gentz, Salomon Maimon, and Friedrich Schleiermacher.

The third woman in this remarkable trio was Dorothea Mendelssohn, daughter of the philosopher. She married the Jewish businessman Simon Veit and is the mother of the well-known painter Philip Veit. Dorothea left Simon and became the mistress and later the wife of the Romantic literary historian and critic Friedrich Schlegel. Like most of the children of Moses Mendelssohn, she converted to Christianity, first becoming a protestant and later a Catholic. In addition to being an accomplished hostess, she translated the works of Madame de Stael into German and wrote fiction. Her unfinished novel *Florentin* reflects the trend of the typical romantic fiction of the day.

By the twentieth century, Jewish women in Germany were gaining ground, freer to pursue endeavors once closed to them. In literature, for example, a number of German Jewish women achieved eminence. Among them are Else Lasker-Schüler, often referred to as Germany's greatest Expressionist poet; Nelly Sachs, recipient of the 1966 Nobel Prize in Literature; and Anna Seghers, author of some of Germany's most engrossing novels of social protest. All three were born and reared in Germany; and all three were forced to leave their native land when the Nazis took power.

The first, Else Lasker-Schüler (born in Elberfeld, 1876, died in Jerusalem, 1945), was the daughter of a Jewish banker and architect and the granddaughter of a rabbi. In 1889, the family moved to Berlin, and Else soon became attracted to literature, especially poetry. In 1902, when she was twenty-six, her first volume of poetry entitled *Styx* was published. It made such an impression on critics and readers alike that she was called the swan of Israel and the modern Sappho. With her new renown, she became one of the leading lights in the bohemian literary and artistic circles of the capital.

Her marriage, to a doctor named Lasker, ended, and she married the art critic Herwarth Walden. As editor of the journal *Sturm*, Walden was well known to Else and her peers, and the couple became the center of a group of Berlin's most prominent writers and artists. Their friends included such prominent painters as Franz Marc and Oskar Kokoschka, and the famous poets Richard Dehmel, Franz Werfel, and Karl Kraus.

Else's Judaism was important to her both as a person and a poet. One of her best-known volumes of poetry is *Hebrew Ballads*, which was published in 1913. When Hitler came to power, she left Germany and went directly to Jerusalem, where she lived out her life. Her last major work, *Das Hebraeerland,* was written there.

Poet and translator Nelly Sachs was different both as an individual and as a writer. Born in Berlin in 1891, she was the only daughter of a Jewish manufacturer. Unlike Else Lasker-Schüler, who led the colorful, unsettled life of a bohemian and was frequently on the edge of poverty, Nelly Sachs led a quiet, cultured life. She grew up in a villa in a fashionable section of Berlin and was educated by private tutors. Her adult years were devoted to music and writing. Nelly Sach's first work, *Legenden und Erzählungen* ("Legends and Tales") came out in 1931 when she was thirty years old.

Over the years, she developed a rich correspondence with the Swedish novelist Selma Lagerlöf who, in 1909, had been the first woman to receive the Nobel Prize in Literature. After the Nazis took power in Germany, Nelly turned to Selma for help, and through her friend's good offices was able to emigrate to Sweden in 1940. There she wrote some of her most moving poetry, much of it mediations on the sufferings of German Jews during the war. *In den Wohnungen das Todes* ("In the

Apartments of Death") appeared in 1947. In 1966, her collection *Die Suchende* ("The Seekers") was published, and that same year she was awarded the Nobel. Her most celebrated work, *O Die Schornsteine* ("O, the Chimneys"), came out the following year, and *Lieden Israels* ("Israel's Sufferings") was published in 1969. Many of her collections were brought out in Germany after the war. Nelly Sachs died in Jerusalem in 1970.

Novelist Anna Seghers was a powerful intellect drawn by a diversity of interests. Born into a middle-class Jewish family in Mainz in 1900, her real name was Netty Reiling Rádvanyi; Anna Seghers, her nom de plume. She studied art history at the university in Cologne and received a Ph.D. in 1924 with her thesis, *Jews and Judaism in the Work of Rembrandt.*

Soon after she left the university, her interests turned to writing fiction. But unlike many of the women writers of the day, her novels were not stories of love and social teas. Politically, she was left wing, and her novels are stories of oppression, protest, and rebellion. Her first, *The Revolt of the Fishermen*, came out in 1929 and catapulted her to renown when it won the prestigious Kleist award in literature.

In 1933, she moved to Paris and, when France fell to the Nazis, she fled to Mexico. During her years of exile, she thrived as a novelist. *The Seventh Cross* (1939), among her most famous works, tells the gripping story of a communist who manages to escape from a concentration camp. Her 1942 novel, *Transit*, recounts the life of a forced emigré.

At the end of the war, Anna returned to Germany and chose the newly partitioned East Berlin as her home. In 1963, the diversity of her interests was again demonstrated when her study of Dostoevskii and Tolstoi was published. Anna Seghers lived into her 80s and died in 1983, a celebrated author.

Our next trio—Rosa Luxemburg, Edith Stein, and Hannah Arendt—are perhaps the most illustrious, not only among German Jewish women, but among men and women everywhere. All of them received Ph.D.'s in philosophy, and all were totally dedicated to their ideas. Prolific writers themselves, they have inspired an extensive literature, including biographies and books and essays discussing their ideas and the contributions they made to philosophy, politics, social theory, economics, and religion.

Rosa Luxemburg was born the same year as Lenin, 1871. Strictly speaking, she was not German, for she was born in Zamosc, which then was part of Russian Poland, but she became a German citizen and spent most of her active life in Germany. Rosa was a woman of slight build and great passion from a well-to-do, cosmopolitan merchant family. Brilliant and spirited, she went to the girl's *gymnasium* in Warsaw and graduated at sixteen, at the top of her class. A gold medal usually went with such a distinction, but the *gymnasium* refused to award it to Rosa, citing her resistance to authority: the year before, when she was only fifteen, she had joined the socialist underground.

At the age of nineteen, she had to flee the country to avoid arrest and went to Switzerland, where she entered the university at Zurich. An outstanding student, she received two doctorates from Zurich, one in philosophy and one in law, in 1897.

During her student days in Switzerland, Rosa Luxemburg continued to be active in revolutionary politics and became one of the leaders of the circle of Polish socialist emigrés. In 1892, she helped to found the Polish Socialist Party; and two years later, she led the wing that would break off to become the Social Democratic Party of Poland. An excellent and fiery speaker, she was also a gifted writer and edited the Polish-language journal *Worker's Cause*. Although she was still a young woman and had no official position, she was sent as a delegate to the Congress of the Second International in Zurich, where her brilliance, combined with her oratorical skill, made a deep impression. She never lost her interest in the revolutionary cause in Poland, or in the Russian revolutions of 1905 and 1917.

Finding life as a political emigré in Switzerland too confining, Rosa moved to Paris, where she met and befriended a number of prominent socialists, and for a brief time became involved with French revolutionary politics. But France was not the center of political thought; Germany was and, in 1897, at the age of twenty-seven, she emigrated to the native country of Marx and Engels. In order to safely pursue her political activities, she knew she would need German citizenship, and so she proposed a "marriage of convenience" to the son of an old German socialist family of her acquaintance, Gustav Luebeck. The two never lived together, and she never used his name.

Luxemburg quickly became known both as a popular orator and a dedicated party worker. She soon emerged as one of the most forceful and influential leaders in Germany's Social Democratic Party, which was beginning to play a leading role in the political life of the country. As a Marxist, she belonged to the left wing of the party and was staunchly opposed by the moderate revisionist members who dominated the German socialist movement. During this time, she contributed regularly to the Marxist journals *Neue Zeit* and *Vorwerts* and taught Marxian economics at the party's Training School. Her book, *Social Reform or Revolution* (1899) is typical of her political thought at the time, advocating revolution over gradual political and economic reform.

Although the majority of German socialists supported their country's involvement in World War I, Luxemburg saw the war as a struggle between imperialist powers and became an ardent pacifist. She was frequently arrested for her antiwar activities, and the prowar stance of many of her socialist friends sent her into a deep despair. Because of this and other differences with her fellow socialists she founded the Spartacus League with Karl Liebknecht in 1917. After the Russian Revolution, she became one of the leaders of the newly established Communist Party of Germany.

In January of 1919, Rosa Luxemburg and Liebknecht were arrested, and as they were being taken off to prison, they were murdered by Prussian officers. She was not yet thirty-eight years old.

Remembered as a martyr and a courageous revolutionary, her letters, written mostly during her prison stays, are still widely read. Her writings, such as *The Russian Revolution* and *Leninism or Marxism*, continued to have a good deal of influence. During the 1960s, Rosa Luxemburg's idealism and self sacrifice inspired a new generation of German revolutionaries.

Edith Stein was as different in temperament and outlook from Luxemburg as anyone could possibly be. Born in Breslau to a traditional middle-class Jewish family in 1891, she lost her father, a merchant, when she was very young. She and her seven siblings were brought up by their mother, a religious woman who would never quite get over the fact that her daughter became a Christian.

A sensitive and intelligent child, Edith was an eager student who excelled in German literature and history. After graduating from the lyceum in 1911, she studied psychology at Breslau University. But the field was dominated by pragmatism then, and she became dissatisfied with her studies. After two years, she transferred to Göttingen University and the study of philosophy under Edmund Husserl. She eventually became his assistant. Husserl, along with the Catholic convert and phenomenologist Max Scheler, greatly influenced the young Edith Stein.

Edith Stein's studies were interrupted by the outbreak of World War I. In order to share the danger and hardships suffered by many of her male classmates, she served as a volunteer in a military hospital, where she formed some close friendships with Christians. The experience of the war years, as well as her relationship with Christian friends, increasingly turned her thoughts away from philosophical idealism and toward religion. After the war, instead of pursuing her academic career, she returned to Breslau and dedicated herself to study and meditation. In 1921, during this period of doubt and crisis, Edith happened upon the autobiography of the sixteenth-century Carmelite nun, St. Theresa of Avila, one of the principal Catholic saints and a genuine mystic. She found the book so fascinating, she sat up all night reading it. By morning, she felt that conversion was the path she must take. On January 1, 1922, when she was thirty years old, she was baptized as a Catholic and chose Theresia as her Christian name.

Edith Theresia then set her sights on entering a Carmelite convent, but her priest advised her to use her considerable intellectual powers in the world. She agreed, partly because she felt that it would be too much of a shock for her mother if, having left the Jewish faith, she also immediately became a nun. Instead, she became a teacher at the Dominican Lyceum of St. Magdalene for girls in Speyer, where she taught from 1922 to 1931. In this time, she also wrote a book on the phenomenology of Husserl and the philosophy of St. Thomas Aquinas.

In 1932, she was appointed docent at the German Institute for Scientific Paedagogy in Münster. But this promising beginning of her academic career came to nothing, for she was dismissed a year after Hitler came to power. With a secular teaching career abruptly closed to her, she returned to her original Catholic aspiration and entered the Carmelite convent in Cologne, receiving the name Theresia Benedicta á Cruce.

Filled with a deep, mystical faith, Edith Stein embraced her new life. She wrote: "If the times were not otherwise so sad—I would be grateful to them [the Nazis] because they have finally opened the way for me."[3] Her only regret was that this meant a final break with her family, particularly her mother, who could neither understand nor condone her decision. Deeply troubled as well by the fate of the Jewish people, she petitioned for a private audience with Pope Pius XI, in hopes she could persuade him to issue an encyclical clarifying the Church's relationship to Judaism and its support of the Jews, but the request was denied. Although she had been estranged from Judaism ever since her teenage years, she took great pride in the fact that she belonged to the very people from whom Jesus had come and felt a kinship with the Jewish people. She was also interested in the Zionist settlements in Palestine, and had even thought of going there to join the Carmelites. (Had she done so, it would have saved her life.)

Although the life of a Carmelite nun was normally peaceful, Edith Stein was profoundly affected by the terrible events which were taking place around her. Her mother died in her old age of cancer, and her brothers and sisters and their families suffered from the Nazi persecutions. Eventually most of them escaped, emigrating to the United States, Norway, and Columbia. Until 1938, she herself had been protected by the Carmelites, although her major work *Endliches und Ewiges Sein*, could not be published in Germany because of her Jewish background. After Kristallnacht, she felt that her presence would be too great on her sisters and had herself transferred to the Carmelite convent in Echt in Holland. There, she wrote *The Science of the Cross*.

In 1940, the Nazis conquered Holland. In 1942, over the protests of the Catholic Bishop of Holland, Dutch Jews were rounded up for deportation to the death camps. The Carmelites arranged to protect Edith Stein by sending her to the Carmelite house in Paquier, Switzerland, but she refused to go without her sister Rosa, who had also joined the order. Before this could be managed, both women were arrested and sent to a Dutch concentration camp.

Even at this hour, when she could see the suffering that lay ahead, she was sustained by her deep religious faith; survivors who met her in the camp have born witness to her inner peace and serenity. Comforting those in despair and looking after the children whose mothers were too shattered to function, she accepted her fate as the will of God. At the moment of her arrest, she had said to her sister, "Come, we go for our people."[4] To Edith Stein, the road she traveled was, in a sense, the *via dolorosa* of the crucifixion, a road which led to redemption and everlasting life, and not a mean ingless path of destruction. On August 7, 1942, she was transported to Poland. It is believed that she was gassed at Auschwitz two days later.

Edith Stein's true stature did not become known to the larger world until after the war, when her suppressed works were published. In 1948, the first Edith Stein biography was published and an Edith Stein Archive was established in Cologne. In 1962, the first steps in the long, slow process of her canonization began. The official papers were finally readied and sent to Rome in 1972. Five years later, the Congregation of Sainthood examined her writings and, in 1980, German bishops asked the pope to initiate the final stage of sanctification. That process was begun in 1981, but at the time of this writing it has not yet been completed.

Hannah Arendt, who was born in Hanover in 1906, never met Edith Stein and was too young to have known Rosa Luxemburg, but she had certain connections with both. On the one hand, her mother was a lifelong socialist whose idol was Rosa Luxemburg; and on the other, she studied under Husserl whose assistant Edith Stein had been. Aside from these connections, however, her life, personality, and temperament could not have been more different.

Hannah was a gifted child who grew up in Königsberg in eastern Prussia and attended the lyceum there. After she graduated, she studied philosophy from 1924 to 1928, first in Marburg under Martin Heidegger, then with Edmund Husserl in Freiburg, and finally with Karl

251

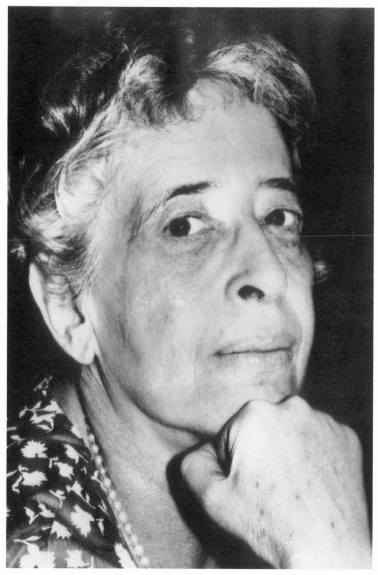

HANNAH ARENDT

Jaspers in Heidelberg, where she received her Ph.D. in 1928. Her relationship to Heidegger was not only academic; the two became lovers, but she broke off the affair when Heidegger welcomed the Nazis and accepted the rectorship of Freiburg University under Hitler. A genuine intellectual with a sharp, penetrating mind, she was raised in the tradition of German idealistic philosophy. Kant was her favorite philosopher and Jaspers, her mentor and friend. Her Ph.D. thesis, *Der Liebesbegriff bei St Augustin*, was published in Berlin in 1929.

Hannah Arendt's first book, completed in 1933, is an account of the life of Rahel Levin Varnhagen. Titled *Rahel Varnhagen*, it draws on Rahel's letters and other writings to paint an intimate portrait of the famous hostess as an intellectual, a Jew, and a center of the German Romantic movement. That same year, Hitler came to power, and she was arrested by the Gestapo and charged with harboring Communists. At this very time, she had been engaged in a linguistic analysis of vulgar Anti-Semitic expressions, a work she had undertaken at the request of her Zionist friend Kurt Blumenthal.

She spent eight days in jail, and upon her release left the country. She first settled in Paris, where she worked for a Zionist youth group which was trying to rescue Jewish children, and married Günther Anders, a fellow refugee. That marriage ended, and she wed Heinrich Blücher, a non-Jewish German radical who had been a participant in the Spartacus uprising in Berlin. After the Nazi conquest of France in 1940, she was again arrested and this time was interned in the enemy alien camp at Gurs. She managed to get out and, with her mother and husband, emigrated to the United States in 1941.

Hannah Arendt's early years in America were difficult ones, for she was a woman in her late thirties with an imperfect command of English and no immediately marketable skills. Nevertheless, she was able to get a job with the Conference on Jewish Relations; she also became a contributor to the *Aufbau*, a German Jewish weekly published in New York. She was not a Marxist, but she had left-wing sympathies. She was also sympathetic to Zionism, to the extent of viewing Palestine as a home for the Jews who were escaping from Europe. However, what she advocated was not a Jewish state but a federation of Jews and Arabs who, she hoped, would live together in peace and harmony.

As her English improved, Arendt began to make a place for herself in the intellectual world of New York. She became an editor at Schocken publishers in 1946, and then a contributor to *The Nation* and *Partisan Review*. Her circle of American friends grew and included editor and author Dwight Macdonald, essayist and novelist Mary McCarthy, and poet W. H. Auden. In 1950, she became a U.S. citizen.

The following year, with the publication of her *Origins of Totalitarianism*, Hannah Arendt became established as one of the major political philosophers in the West. An ambitious attempt to explain the rise of dictators and the appalling crimes committed in that period of the twentieth century, the work is filled with new insights and reflects the sum of her philosophical and political knowledge. In it, she argues that there was little difference between Hitler's Germany and Stalin's Russia, both of which were totalitarian states, with one emphasizing race and the other, class. In taking this view, she seemed to endorse the Cold War, which was probably one of the reasons the book created such a stir and won so large an audience. The book led to appointments as a lecturer and Guggenheim fellow from 1952 to 1953 and visiting professor at the University of California at Berkeley in 1955. She also continued to write for magazines and, in 1958, her next important work, *The Human Condition*, was published. The following year, her academic career soared. She became a full professor at Princeton University, and in 1960 she added to that the position of visiting professor of government at Columbia University, New York.

In 1961, she wrote a long essay, "Eichmann in Jerusalem: A Report on the Banality of Evil," which appeared in *The New Yorker Magazine*. The work proved to be extremely controversial, and it was bitterly denounced by Jews throughout the world. Two truckloads of angry letters were delivered to the offices of *The New Yorker*; after a lengthier version of it was published in book form in 1963 as *Eichmann in Jerusalem*, virtually every review was critical. The two points that aroused the greatest resentment were, first, that the European Jewish communities had not only collaborated with the Nazis by providing lists of Jews and their property to the authorities, but they had also gone to their death like lambs to slaughter; and, second, that Eichmann, far from being a unique monster, was an ordinary bureaucrat—hence, the "Banality of Evil" in the essay's title. Another point that angered many was her characterization of Leo Baeck, the saintly last rabbi of Berlin, as a Jewish *führer*, a passage which she herself deleted in the 1965 paperback edition of the book.

The attention that the Eichmann book received overshadowed another important work of 1963, her thoughtful study *On Revolution*. That same year, Arendt accepted an appointment as full professor at the University of Chicago. She remained there until 1967, when she returned to New York as professor at the New School of Social Research. In 1968, her book *Men in Dark Times* was brought out, and 1969 saw the publication of another major work, *On Violence*.

But the book on Eichmann continued to haunt her until the end of her life. However much she went forward to contribute new and fresh insights in other areas of political theory, the critics of *Eichmann in Jerusalem* continued to see that as her defining work and refused to let go of it. Many of her old friends left her on account of it, and not even her publisher came to her defense. As important as her other writings in fact are, Hannah Arendt never in her lifetime regained the eminence she had known before 1963.[5]

Still in her early sixties, she died in New York in 1970 and was buried in Annandale-on-Hudson, New York, near Bard College, where her husband had been a professor.

Hannah Arendt was one of the last German Jews to receive their intellectual training in Germany and write in the German language. While not a religious Jew, she was keenly aware of her Jewish heritage. When she spoke at Heidelberg University after the war, she began her lecture by announcing, "Ich bin eine Deutsche Jüdin," a remark which was greeted with ringing applause. Most of Hannah Arendt's career unfolded in the New World. It is probably no exaggeration to say that, today, the German Jewish community is larger in America than it is in Germany itself.

At the end of the twentieth century, the vital, productive symbiosis of German and Jewish thought and culture has ceased. But the extraordinary men and women it produced will live on in their bequest.

NOTES

[1] It is available in English. See M. Lowenthal, ed., *The Memoirs of Glückel of Hameln* (New York: Harper, 1932).

[2] H. M. Sachar, *The Course of Modern Jewish History* (Cleveland: World Publishing, 1958), 140-41.

[3] Waltrand Hebstrith, *Edith Stein, Ein Neue Lebensbild* (Freiburg, 1983), 49 (author's translation). See also: Edith Stein, *Life in a Jewish Family: Her Unfinished Autobiographical Account,* in Edith Stein, *Works* (English), vol. 1. (Washington, D.C.: ICS Publications, 1986). An English language edition is available: Waltrand Herbstrith, *Edith Stein, A Biography* (San Francisco: Harper & Row, 1985).

[4] *Ibid.*, 60.

[5] Among recent studies, we recommend: Maurizio Passerin d'Entreves, *The Political Philosophy of Hannah Arendt,* (London, New York: Routledge, 1994); and Elisabeth Young-Bruehl, *Hannah Arendt for Love of the World* (New Haven: Yale University Press, c1982).

SELECTED
BIBLIOGRAPHIES

General Histories of the Jewish People

Baron, Salo Wittmayer. *A Social and Religious History of the Jews,* 2d. ed., rev. and enl. New York, Columbia University Press, 1993.

Dubunow, Simon Markevich. *An Outline of Jewish History,* 3 vols. New York: Max N. Maisel, 1925-19.

Graetz, Heinrich. *A History of the Jews,* 6 vols. Philaelphia: Jewish Publication Society, 1891-1898.

_____. *The Structure of Jewish History and Other Essays.* New York: Jewish Theological Seminary of America/ Ktav Publishing House, 1975.

Jacobs, Joseph. *Jewish Contributions to Civilization.* Philadelphia: The Conant Press, 1920.

259

Johnson, Paul. *A History of the Jews.* New York: Harper & Row, 1987.

Marcus, Jacob Rader. *The Jew in the Medieval World.* A Source Book. Cincinnati: Hebrew Union College Press, 1990.

Roth, Cecil. *The Jewish Contribution to Civilisation.* London: Macmillan, 1938.

_____. *A Short History of the Jews,* 5th ed., rev. and enl. London: East & West Library, 1969.

_____. *A History of the Jews from Earliest Times,* rev. ed. New York: Schocken Books, 1970.

Sachar, Abram Leon. *A History of the Jews,* 5th ed., rev. and enl. New York: Knopf, 1965.

Sacher, Howard Morley. *The Course of Modern Jewish History,* rev. ed. New York: Vintage Books, 1990.

General Books on German Jews

Adler, H.G. *The Jews in Germany: From the Enlightenment to National Socialism.* Notre Dame, In.: U. of Notre Dame Press, 1969.

Bach, Hans Israel. *The German Jew: A Synthesis of Judaism and Western Civilization, 1730-1930.* Oxford and New York: Oxford University Press, published for the Littman Library, 1984.

Ehrlich, Ernst Ludwig. *Geschichte der Juden in Deutschland.* Dusseldorf: Padagogischer Verlag Schwann, 1961, c1954.

Elbogen, Ismar. *Die Geschichte der Juden in Deutschland.* Hamburg: Europaische Verlagsanstalt, 1993, c1935.

Gay, Ruth. *The Jews of Germany: A Historical Portrait.* Introduction lby Peter Gay. New Haven, Conn.: Yale University Press, 1992.

Kampmann, W. *Deutsche und Juden.* Frankfurt: Fischer Taschenbuch Verlag, 1979, c1963.

Kaznelson, Siegmund, ed. *Juden im deutschen Kulturbereich: ein Sammelwerk,* 3rd ed. Berlin: Judischer Verlag, 1962.

Liptzin, Solomon, *Germany's Stepchildren.* Cleveland and Philadelphia: Jewish Publication Society of America, 1961, c1944.

Lowenthal, Marvin. *The Jews of Germany: A Story of Sixteen Centuries.* New York: Russell & Russell, 1970, c1936.

Marcus, Jacob Rader. *The Rise and Destiny of the German Jew.* New York: Ktav Publishing House, 1973, c1934.

Mosse, George Lachmann. *Germans and Jews: The Right, The Left, and The Search for a "Third Force" in pre-Nazi Germany.* Detroit: Wayne State University Press, 1987, c1970.

_____. *German Jews Beyond Judaism.* Bloomington: Indiana University Press / Cincinnati: Hebrew Union College Press, 1985.

Richarz, Monica, Stella Rosenfield, and Sidney Rosenfield, ed., *Jewish Life in Germany: Memoirs from Three Centuries.* Bloomington: Indiana University Press, 1991. (Translated and abridged version of *Judisches Leben in Deutschland,* 3 vols. 1979.)

Stern, Fritz Richard. *Dreams and Delusions: The Drama of Germany History*. New York: Vintage Books, 1989.

Weiner Library. *German Jewry: Its History, Life, and Culture*, 2 vols. London: Vallentine, Mitchell, 1958.

Books on German Jews During the Nazi Period

Leo Baeck Institute. *Year Book,* vols. I–XXXIX. London: East & West Libraries; or London: Secker & Warburg; published for the Leo Baeck Institute, 1956-1994.

Engelmann, Bernt. *Germany Without Jews*. New York and Toronto: Bantam Books, 1984.

Heilbut, Anthony. *Exiled in Paradise: German Refugee Artists and Intellectuals in America, from the 1930s to the Present*. Boston: Beacon Press: 1984.

Heuberger, Rachel, and Helga Krohn. *Hinaus aus dem Ghetto* (Juden im Frankfurt am Main, 1800-1950). Frankfurt am Main: Fischer, 1988.

Huttenbach, Henry R. *The Destruction of the Jewish Community of Worms, 1933-1945*. New York: Memorial Committee of Jewish Victims of Nazism from Worms, 1981.

The Jews in Nazi Germany: The Factual Record of Their Persecution by the National Socialists. New York: American Jewish Committee, 1983, c1933.

The Jews in Nazi Germany: A Handbook of Facts Regarding Their Present Situation. New York: H. Fertig, 1982, c1935.

Encyclopedias

The Concise Jewish Encyclopedia. New York: New American Library, 1980.

Encyclopedia Judaica, 16 vols. Jerusalem and New York: Macmillan, 1972.

Jewish Encyclopedia, 12 vols. New York: Ktav Publishing House, 1925.

The Junior Jewish Encyclopedia, 5th rev. ed. New York: Shengold Publishers, 1963.

The New Standard Jewish Encyclopedia, new rev. ed. London: W.H. Allen, 1970.

The Standard Jewish Encyclopedia, rev. ed. Jerusalem: Massadah Publishers, 1966.

The Universal Jewish Encyclopedia, 10 vols. New York: Universal Jewish Encyclopedia, Inc., 1939-49.

PICTURE CREDITS

Hannah Arendt, page 252: Topham/The Image Works.

Martin Buber, page 50: courtesy of the Leo Baeck Institute, N.Y.

Albert Einstein, page 96: Topham/The Image Works.

Erich Fromm, page 114: courtesy of The Crossroad Publishing Company.

Heinrich Heine, page 184: Shumsky Archives/The Image Works

Ferdinand Lassalle, page 150: New York Public Library Picture Collection.

Karl Marx, page 70: Topham/The Image Works.

Erich Mendelsohn, page 202: Lotte Jacobi Collection, Dimond Library, University of New Hampshire.

Felix Mendelssohn Bartholdy, page 220: Image Works Archives.

Moses Mendelssohn, page 34: courtesy of the Leo Baeck Institute, New York.

Walter Rathenau, page 168: Topham/The Image Works.

Mayer Amschel Rothschild, page 137: New York Public Library Picture Collection.